BLESSED

Eight Ways Christians Change Culture

Also by Dr. Jim Denison

The Daily Article email newsletter is news discerned differently every Monday through Friday. Subscribe for free at DenisonForum.org.

To Follow in His Footsteps:
A Daily Devotional through the Holy Sites of Israel

Bright Hope for Tomorrow:
How Jesus' Parables Illuminate Our Darkest Days

Respectfully, I Disagree:
How to Be a Civil Person in an Uncivil Time

The Greater Work:
How Prayer Positions You
to Receive All that Grace Intends to Give

7 Deadly Sins:
How Our Oldest Temptations
Can Lead You from Vice to Virtue

Making Sense of Suffering:
7 Biblical Ways to Help Hurting People

Biblical Insight to Tough Questions: Vols. 1–7

How Does God See America?

Request these books at DenisonForum.org/store

CONTENTS

Acknowledgments

Thomas à Kempis wisely advised us: "Do not be influenced by the importance of the writer, and whether his learning be great or small, but let the love of pure truth draw you to read. Do not inquire, Who said this? but pay attention to what is said."

While I certainly agree that you should not be influenced by my "importance" (whatever it may be), I want you to know about those members of our ministry team whose contributions have been vital to "what is said" in this small volume.

Ryan Denison, my oldest son and research assistant, contributed concepts and helpful critique to the introduction and several of the chapters. Blake Atwood edited my words once again with incisive excellence. Minni Elkins provided stellar proofreading, as usual. Melissa Tjarks has overseen the project from conception to completion with grace and professionalism. Emily Tomasella provided graphics support that transformed my word documents into the attractive volume in your hands. And Chris Elkins, my chief of staff, directed our team with his usual servant heart and outstanding leadership.

It is a great honor to partner with them in this ministry.

And to share our collective work with you.

Soli Deo gloria.

Introduction

Pick an issue in the news. Whether you thought first of abortion, racial prejudice, the LGBTQ agenda, poverty, euthanasia, or something else, now ask yourself: Is our culture moving closer to or further away from God's word on this issue?

Consider racial discrimination.

Five decades after the Civil Rights Act of 1964 ended segregation in public places and banned employment discrimination on the basis of race, color, religion, sex, or national origin, we might think American society is making great progress toward racial equality. But according to a recent Pew Research Center poll, a majority of Americans believe race relations in the United States are bad. Of those, about seven in ten say things are getting even worse.

What about poverty?

We might think that the longest stock market expansion in American history would translate into good news on this issue. While the percentage of Americans living in poverty has declined from over 15 percent in 2010 to 12.3 percent in 2017, the poverty rate for all infants rose from 17.2 percent in 2016 to 20.2 percent in 2017. For black infants, the rate escalated from 28.5 percent to 34.4 percent. Minorities had higher poverty rates than non-Hispanic whites, and child poverty is among the highest in the industrialized world.

What about abortion?

We might note the report from the US Centers for Disease Control and Prevention that abortions in the United States have dropped to their lowest level in ten years. However, this "lower" level still reflects the deaths of more than 638,000 babies. And the movement to legitimize and even celebrate abortion continues to escalate.

When we turn to issues such as pornography, sex outside of heterosexual marriage, religious liberty, and euthanasia, our moral descent is even clearer.

What is the answer?

A movement of culture-changing Christians

In his Sermon on the Mount, Jesus declared to his followers: "You are the salt of the earth . . . You are the light of the world" (Matthew 5:13, 14).

You is plural, including all Christians. *Are* is in the present tense, describing a fact, not a prediction or a supposition. *The* makes it clear that we are the *only* salt and light of the world.

Salt purifies; light dispels darkness.

From our Lord's statement, we can know that if our culture is decaying and darkening, the answer is for God's people to become the change agents he intends us to be. In short, what America needs most is a movement of culture-changing Christians.

Denison Ministries exists to be a catalyst for such a movement. Each of our ministry brands uniquely contributes to this calling:

- **First15** leads believers into a daily, empowering encounter with our Lord at First15.org.

- **Christian Parenting** equips parents to raise children to know and love the Lord at ChristianParenting.org.

- **Janet Denison's** teaching ministry helps believers apply God's word to their lives at JanetDenison.org.

- **Denison Forum** equips Christians to discern news differently by engaging cultural issues with biblical truth at DenisonForum.org.

Our collective purpose is to "equip the saints for the work of ministry" (Ephesians 4:12) so they can use their influence to change the culture for Christ.

When I discuss this mission, however, people often ask me: What does a culture-changing Christian look like? What characteristics define someone God is using to impact the culture for Jesus?

Before our Lord defined our calling as salt and light, he first gave us eight statements that answer our question. The Beatitudes tell us precisely how Christians who are changing the culture live—the values and commitments that motivate and inspire them.

As we explore these timeless principles together, our purpose is simple: to align our lives with these eight principles so fully that they define our character and empower our influence.

When we do, we will be the salt and light our Lord desires and our culture desperately needs.

The sermon that changed the world

One of the primary emphases in Matthew's gospel is helping Christians learn how to be better followers of Christ while guiding others to do the same. To that end, he bookends Jesus' teaching ministry with two passages: The Sermon on the Mount (Matthew 5–7) and the Great Commission (Matthew 28:18–20). The God who inspired Matthew's writing was clearly concerned with reminding us that his Son came to accomplish even more than securing our eternal salvation.

The day we trust Christ as our Savior and Lord is the start of a relationship that will extend throughout all of eternity. Too often, though, we make the mistake of thinking that eternity doesn't start until we get to heaven. The truth is that we are called to invest in our relationship with our Father in this life as well as in the life to come, which means becoming more like Christ every single day.

What does such a lifestyle look like?

It has often been said that Christians are meant to represent God's hands and feet to the world around us. Yet that mission is doomed to fail if we cannot represent his heart and mind as well. The religious leaders in the time of Christ placed the utmost importance on the observance of God's laws and created safeguard upon safeguard to ensure that people would not transgress them. The gospels, however, are filled with examples of how God desires more from his people.

Fortunately, he also left us with a clear guide on how to serve him with our hearts and minds as well as with our actions.

In the Sermon on the Mount, Jesus essentially gives us his systematic ethic for how to be his disciples. And whether one believes it was given as one sermon or is rather a summary of his teachings, it represents the core of what he taught across three years of public ministry.

The sermon covers a wide range of topics that encompass nearly every facet of what Jesus expects of those who claim to follow him. As St. Augustine notes, the Sermon represents "a perfect standard of the Christian life."

To this end, it's fitting that Matthew began his record of Jesus' teaching ministry with this sermon. He wanted his readers to see this message as the lens through which we should understand the rest of our Lord's teachings and to note that it lays the foundation for understanding all that follows.

It must have come as a shock when Jesus began his sermon by stating, "Blessed are the poor in spirit, for theirs is the kingdom of heaven." When he continued with a series of seven additional blessings, all of which were countercultural to the society of his day (and ours as well), it would have been impossible to avoid the response of those who first heard him: "The crowds were astonished at his teaching, for he was teaching them as one who had authority, and not as their scribes" (Matthew 7:28–29).

You see, contrary to the way in which the Law was presented by most religious leaders of his time, Jesus began his moral instruction by focusing on *character* rather than commands. Until we understand why, we'll never fully grasp the gravity of all the instruction that comes after.

Even if we somehow managed to keep every command found in this sermon but did not exhibit the characteristics described in its first twelve verses, we would never fully experience the blessing of God in our lives. Nor would we become the salt and light our culture needs.

"Blessed are the . . . ."

Let's begin by noting the manner in which Jesus states the "Beatitudes" (from the Latin phrase for "blessings"). While I doubt many will read this book hoping for a grammar lesson (I know I wouldn't), there are a few key pieces of information that are vital if we want to understand fully all that Christ teaches in these verses.

First: What Jesus offers us in the Beatitudes is a guide to the kinds of blessings only God can provide. It's a blessedness that transcends our circumstances, a joy and peace that the world can neither give nor take. We'll learn more about those blessings as we look at each verse in greater detail; but, from the start, we must acknowledge that what the Lord offers is something only he can deliver.

Second: Jesus says, "Blessed are." He does not say "Blessed were," when times were better. Nor does he say "Blessed will be," when your current troubles pass. He says, "Blessed are." The blessings that God uniquely offers are available to you each and every moment of your life. Those who live with the character described in these verses will know and abide in a kind of blessing that too often we mistakenly believe is reserved for heaven (or, at least, for our more peaceful times on earth).

Third: Jesus states, "Blessed are *the*." In seven of the eight Beatitudes, Jesus begins by using some form of this definitive article to describe those who are blessed, the only exception being when he personalizes those who are persecuted in the final Beatitude. By starting with some variation of "Blessed are *the/those*," Jesus demonstrates that these characteristics form the *only* path to the blessing God wants us to have.

There is no other way because there could not be another way. The remnants of our fallen nature make it too difficult to otherwise live every day with the kind of character Jesus describes in these verses.

So, we've seen that Jesus was emphatic about both the uniqueness and the necessity of these characteristics for those who want to experience the kind of blessing only God can provide. But are all of them necessary, or can we experience enough blessing to get by if we just focus on the few that come easiest to us?

A systematic ethic

It's human nature to gravitate toward that which we feel adequate to accomplish. Given that the idea of shaping our character to conform with each of the traits espoused in the Beatitudes is an inherently overwhelming task, it will take a conscious effort to avoid focusing on those that come more naturally while paying less attention to those that require more effort on our part.

It's important to note, however, that Jesus did not intend to give us this option. When Christ began by stating, "Blessed are the poor in spirit, for theirs is the kingdom of heaven" (Matthew 5:3), he laid the foundation upon which the other Beatitudes would be built. We will discover more about why this is true when we discuss verse 3, but the same general principle is true of all the Beatitudes. Each of them describes a component of the Christian life without which our character will fall short of the standard to which Jesus has called us.

Moreover, we cannot consistently practice some of these traits to the exclusion of the rest. For example, those who mourn can only be comforted if they are poor in spirit and therefore open to the kingship of Christ in their lives. The pure in heart will see God because they hunger and thirst for righteousness with a meekness that enables them to entrust every facet of their lives to the Father. Those who are persecuted for righteousness' sake can find the strength to rejoice and be glad because they have learned to see themselves as members of God's kingdom and family.

Such examples could be given for each of the Beatitudes, and this principle will become self-evident after studying each blessing in turn. For now, it is vital that we approach this section of God's word convinced of the absolute necessity of each characteristic Jesus chose to include.

The Beatitudes truly form a systematic ethic for what it means to be a disciple of Christ. Absent this holistic approach, we cannot fully appreciate the kind of life to which we are called.

The nature of blessing

As we've noted, living in accordance with the characteristics described in the Beatitudes is necessary for positioning ourselves to receive the blessings Christ promises. Yet, to fully appreciate this fact means a brief word must first be said as to the nature of these blessings. The same Teacher who offers them also warned us: "In this world you will have tribulation" (John 16:33). Clearly, he did not promise a life free from struggle.

In truth, being blessed as Jesus describes in these verses is not essential to living a happy life. Millions of Americans who have no personal relationship with Jesus would nonetheless say they are happy. At times, living by the Beatitudes can even be counterproductive to a feeling of happiness.

But such a life is not what Jesus wants most for us. Rather, he promises a life of purpose and fulfillment, a sense of well-being that transcends circumstances and makes a genuine difference in the world. In short, what the Beatitudes promise are the necessary blessings to be a force for the kingdom in our culture. If we're honest with ourselves, isn't such significance what we really seek most?

We can momentarily satiate our desire for happiness and peace in any number of ways, many of which are neither wicked nor sinful. Yet, when this brief joy fades, the yearning for something more, for the kind of life Jesus describes in these verses, will always return. The only way to end this cycle is to devote our lives so completely to our Lord and his ways that every moment is saturated with his presence.

Fortunately, such a life is exactly what the Beatitudes are meant to produce. They are, in a sense, Christ's vision for what our lives could be like if we let him be our king. This is not a life of ease, and it will require the kind of self-sacrifice that does not come naturally to us. It is, however, the only way to know the kind of lasting joy and purpose for which we were created. And it is the only way to be the salt and light that will change our culture for God's glory.

CHAPTER 1

DEPEND ON THE SPIRIT

"Blessed are the poor in spirit,
for theirs is the kingdom of heaven."
—Matthew 5:3

Archimedes famously declared, "Give me a lever long enough and a fulcrum on which to place it, and I shall move the world." The ancient physicist and engineer (288–212 BC) would need a very long lever.

Our planet is estimated to weigh around 13,170,000,000,000,000, 000,000,000 pounds. To move it even one-millionth of a meter, it's been estimated that Archimedes would need a lever 8.45 light-years long.

Earth is just one of approximately 1,000,000,000,000,000,000,000,000 planets in the observable universe. And yet, our Creator measures the entire universe in the palm of his hand (Isaiah 40:12).

To change our secularized, post-Christian culture seems a task too daunting for us to accomplish. Reading the news each day can be discouraging and even demoralizing. We're right—you and I cannot convict a single sinner of a single sin or change a single soul. We cannot change even one person, much less our culture.

But God can.

The same Spirit who created the universe (Genesis 1:2) stands ready to recreate any fallen human who turns to Jesus in faith (2 Corinthians 5:17). Our Father will forgive every sin we confess (1 John 1:9) and transform every person who is yielded to his power and purpose (Romans 8:29).

To join him in changing the culture, we must submit our lives to the only power that can change the culture. The first Beatitude is Jesus' invitation to precisely such an empowered, transformative life.

The power of *ptochos*

Greek is a fascinating language. Its vocabulary is considered the richest in the world, with more than five million words. (By contrast, the twenty-volume Oxford English Dictionary contains entries for 171,476 words.)

For example, Greek has two very different words that are translated into English as "poor." One is *penes*, which describes a person who has nothing to spare. This is the family living hand-to-mouth, surviving paycheck to paycheck. But this is not the word in our text.

The first Beatitude employs a different Greek word: *ptochos*, which describes a person who has nothing at all. This is the family that is starving to death, who has no idea where their next meal is coming from.

Translating his words directly, Jesus says, "Blessed are those who are starving to death spiritually." *The Message* puts it: "You're blessed when you're at the end of your rope." The New English Bible says, "Blessed are those who know their need of God." This is the exact opposite of how Jesus' culture and ours measure success.

The Jews of Jesus' day believed that material prosperity was a direct sign of divine blessing. Romans believed the same. People in both cultures wanted as much financial means as they could possess, seeking to be as wealthy and healthy as possible.

None would say that a spiritually starving person is blessed. But that's exactly Jesus' claim.

How is this possible?

Those who recognize their absolute need for God and are not dependent on their own circumstances are the only people positioned to receive blessings from God.

When we note the good in our lives and focus on the role we played in attaining it, a fundamental part of its blessing is the sense of pride and accomplishment we feel as a result. However, such an approach focuses on us more than on our Lord. And it keeps us from making him the king of our lives (more on this in a moment).

By contrast, those who are truly poor in spirit see every blessing through the lens of God's role in their lives. Every bit of good leads them back to his throne, and every experience of blessing fills them with gratitude for their Lord.

They do not ignore the role they played in the process of attaining such good, but the primary emotion they feel is gratitude rather than self-satisfaction. This is a fine line, but its importance cannot be overstated.

Jesus definitively states that the poor in spirit will be blessed because only the poor in spirit have fully embraced the reality that a strong relationship with the Lord—one in which he is the king of their lives—is the greatest blessing we can ever receive. So, what does such kingship entail?

Recognizing God as King

Friedrich Nietzsche claimed that the "will to power" is the basic drive in human nature. In his view, everything we do is motivated by a quest for more power over the world, others, and ourselves.

Nietzsche was right. The essential temptation in human experience is the first temptation in human experience: "You will be like God" (Genesis 3:5). Each of us wants to be our own god. We want to be king of our kingdom, ruler of our world.

It is only when we recognize how broken we are and how desperately we need God that we turn from ourselves to him. Only when we are spiritually starved will we get off the throne of our hearts and elevate him there. Only when we are desperate will we become dependent.

And when we are dependent, we position ourselves to receive all that our Father wants for his children. When we are dependent, we will follow his leading into his "good and acceptable and perfect" will (Romans 12:2). When we are dependent, we will yield to his Spirit's power and direction (Ephesians 5:18).

The kingdom of heaven cannot be experienced in any other way.

This kingdom is referenced more than thirty times in Matthew's gospel. Jesus gave us its most succinct definition when he taught us to pray, "Your kingdom come, your will be done, on earth as it is in heaven" (Matthew 6:10). God's kingdom comes when his will is done. His kingdom comes when he is king.

The poor in spirit recognize that they need God above everything and everyone else. As a result, seeking his will becomes their highest priority because they see doing so as essential to their spiritual survival.

By contrast, at the heart of our moral trajectory today is our culture's drive to be our own god. Postmodern relativism has taught us that there is no such thing as absolute truth (which is an absolute truth claim, by the way). Rather, many believe that truth is what we believe it to be. "No one has the right to force their beliefs on us" is the mantra of the day.

In such a culture, the Bible becomes a diary of religious experiences and God becomes a hobby. Faith moves from being central to society to being peripheral and irrelevant. Some even claim that belief in God is dangerous today.

As a result, we should not be surprised when the kingdom of heaven seems little more than a distant hope for another life.

And while we should expect the lost to embrace such a secular mindset, the greatest tragedy is when this mindset is found within the walls of the church.

Remember that when Jesus first stated that the poor in spirit would be blessed, he spoke most directly to those who claimed to follow him. The Sermon on the Mount has wisdom for all people, but its target audience is us. If we want to see the kingdom of heaven made a more present reality in our culture, then this movement must start with every believer choosing to embrace the kingdom in his or her own life first.

How can we do that today?

Four steps to a solid foundation

"Blessed are the poor in spirit, for theirs is the kingdom of heaven" is foundational to every beatitude that follows. If we do not admit our need of God, we will not obey the words that his Son gave us. We will not heed his principles and live out his truths. And we will not embrace the kind of countercultural mindset that will allow us to experience any of the blessings he longs to give.

So, let's take a look at four practical steps we can take to better embrace the mindset of the poor in spirit.

First, submit to the power of the Holy Spirit.

God's word commands us to "be filled with the Spirit" (Ephesians 5:18). The Greek could be literally translated: "Be continually being controlled by the Spirit." Every Christian is to submit every day to the Spirit's control and empowering.

I want to urge you to begin each day with this commitment. Ask the Lord to bring to mind anything in your life that is hindering his Spirit, then confess what comes to your thoughts. Pray through your plans for the day, asking the Spirit to take control of them. Invite him to lead you, empower you, and use you.

Then walk into the day believing that you are "filled" with the Spirit. When you face temptations or challenges, ask the

Spirit for his help. If you fall to temptation, ask the Spirit to forgive you, cleanse you, and restore you. When you face decisions, ask the Spirit to guide you. When you experience victories, thank the Spirit for blessing you.

The single most important decision culture-changing Christians can make is to be filled with the Spirit each and every day.

Second, measure success spiritually.

Unlike Jesus' culture and ours, the Lord knows that material success is fleeting but spiritual success is eternal. He knows that our souls outlive our bodies, that eternity is longer than today, that heaven is more important than earth. He calls us to measure success by his definitions, not ours.

Determine success by the degree to which God uses you today. Look for work only his Spirit can perform. Seek ways to join him at work in circumstances and in the lives of others. Value the eternal over the temporal, the relational over the material, and that which glorifies God over that which glorifies us.

Third, measure spirituality by dependence on God.

The more we are "poor in spirit"—the more we admit our desperation for God's wisdom, direction, healing, forgiveness, and grace—the more we will have what we need. Reject the cultural lie that you can do anything if you'll only get up earlier, stay up later, work longer, and try harder.

Instead, allow God to direct your time and efforts in a way that maximizes your impact for the kingdom without depleting you in the process.

Fourth, measure dependence by obedience.

When we are truly "poor in spirit," we will do the will of God at any cost. Obedience to his commands will become the only food that truly satisfies our souls and the lens through which we perceive every choice we make. Then we will advance the kingdom of God and make Christ our King.

Conclusion

Of all the beatitudes, this one is not only the most foundational, it is also the most surprising and countercultural—then and today.

So, here's my question: Are you "poor in spirit"?

Do you know how much you need Jesus? Or are you separating Sunday from Monday, the spiritual from the secular, religion from the "real world"? Are you confining the Lord of the universe to part of your life, or are you seeking his will and word for every dimension of your life?

We can get there in one of two ways: through our problems or through our potential.

We can let our challenges drive us to God, getting so far down we have nowhere to look but up. Or we can envision what our lives could be like if we were truly dependent on our King, if his omniscience led us and his omnipotence empowered us.

Think of the difference we could make in our culture if the God of the universe were in complete control of us. Think of the souls that would be saved, the lives that would be changed, the ways God would be glorified if we were "poor in spirit."

C. S. Lewis: "It would seem that Our Lord finds our desires not too strong, but too weak. We are half-hearted creatures, fooling about with drink and sex and ambition when infinite joy is offered us, like an ignorant child who wants to go on making mud pies in a slum because he cannot imagine what is meant by the offer of a holiday at the sea. We are far too easily pleased."

Are you?

Discussion Questions

1. What personal challenges do you face in being "poor in spirit" today?

2. In what ways does our culture make submission to the Holy Spirit difficult?

3. Why is being "filled with the Spirit" vital to your cultural influence today?

CHAPTER 2

REDEEM SUFFERING

*"Blessed are those who mourn,
for they shall be comforted."*
—Matthew 5:4

My father was a Sunday school teacher before he fought
in World War II. He did not attend church services again.
He could not understand how a loving God could allow the
horrors he'd experienced.

I lead study tours to Israel several times each year. Being in
the Holy Land is one of the highlights of my ministry. I love
the Jewish people and love being in their country. But I grieve
for the millions who still grieve for family members lost to the
Holocaust and who do not believe in God as a result.

If we are to be culture-changing Christians, we will be forced to confront the greatest single obstacle to faith for many: the ever-present reality of evil and suffering.

Christianity teaches that God is all knowing, all loving, and all powerful. Why, then, did he allow the Holocaust? Or my father's war experience? Or the pain you are facing today?

This is not a book on apologetics (i.e., methods of defending the faith). If it were, we would pivot to resources intended to equip Christians for responding to the challenge of evil and suffering with biblical truth and practical compassion. (For more here, see my book, *Wrestling with God*, and my website article, *Why does a good God allow an evil world?*)

Instead, we will focus in this chapter on the kind of faith and character we need to show our suffering world that God's knowledge, love, and power are relevant to their deepest needs. When we trust God with our pain and experience his transforming grace and strength, we can then offer others what we have received.

Let's claim God's promise: we will mourn, but we will be comforted. And let's learn to model its assurance for our skeptical culture.

Seek to be "blessed"

We'll begin with some background.

When Jesus launched his public ministry, "his fame spread throughout all Syria, and they brought him all the sick, those afflicted with various diseases and pains, those oppressed by demons, those having seizures, and paralytics, and he healed them. And great crowds followed him from Galilee and the Decapolis, and from Jerusalem and Judea, and from beyond the Jordan" (Matthew 4:24–25).

22

In response, "seeing the crowds, he went up on a mountain, and when he sat down, his disciples came to him. And he opened his mouth and taught them" (Matthew 5:1–2). This happened in the area marked by the Church of the Beatitudes, a Franciscan chapel completed in 1938. Somewhere on this hillside, Jesus preached the most famous sermon of all time.

As we saw in the previous chapter, his first beatitude laid the foundation for all the others: "Blessed are the poor in spirit, for theirs is the kingdom of heaven" (v. 3). To be "poor in spirit" is to know how desperately we need God. When we admit that fact, we make God our king and advance the "kingdom of heaven." Then we are "blessed" with God's best.

The second beatitude begins in the same way: "Blessed." This is a translation of the Greek word *makarios*, meaning "a sense of well-being that transcends circumstances." Our culture offers happiness based on our happenings, but Jesus offers blessedness based on his grace. Our culture offers us what our circumstances can give, but Jesus offers us what no circumstance can give or take.

Don't settle for happiness. Don't settle for what the world can steal. Don't settle for anything but God's best.

How do we experience it? Admit how much we need God, how much he could do with our lives if he were fully our king. Envision what it would be like to be led by his omniscience and empowered by his omnipotence. Then make him king of every dimension of our lives.

Expect to mourn

But such blessedness does not insulate us from suffering. The opposite is true, in fact. The second beatitude does not say, "Blessed are those who might mourn" or "who happen to mourn," but "who mourn." The implication—and the fact—is that everyone will mourn.

"Mourn" translates *penthountes*, which describes a kind of grief so deep that it takes possession of the entire person and cannot be hidden. The Greek translation of Genesis 37 uses the word to describe Jacob's grief upon learning of the supposed death of his son, Joseph (v. 34).

What causes such mourning?

We mourn our losses.

The death of my father at the age of fifty-five is still the great loss of my life. He died ten days before Christmas in 1979. He never saw me married or heard me preach. He never met my sons. He would have been a wonderful grandfather.

What losses are you mourning today?

We mourn our failures.

We all have mistakes in our pasts we would pay a high price to correct. Things we did but should not have done; things we did not do but should have done. People we hurt; opportunities we missed.

I had a friend in high school who took his own life. I will wonder for the rest of my life what I could have done to help him.

What failures are you mourning today?

We mourn our sins.

These are moral failures, things we thought, said, and did that violated the word and will of God. After David committed adultery with Bathsheba and then arranged for the death of her husband, he later said to God, "I know my transgressions, and my sin is ever before me" (Psalm 51:3). We all know the feeling.

What sins are you mourning today?

Expect to be comforted

So, we've seen the mourning side of our beatitude; now let's move to the celebrating side: "for they shall be comforted." The Greek literally means "they shall be encouraged" or "they shall be invited in."

Note that this statement is unconditional: not "they may be comforted" but "they *shall* be comforted." This is a future indicative, the promise of an absolute fact.

And yet, so many in our world mourn but are not comforted. How can God make this promise?

Here's the key: the first beatitude empowers the second. When I admit how much I need God, I bring my grief to him. I don't try to handle it myself. I don't ask other people to do what only God can do. I bring it directly and unconditionally to God. I make him the king of it.

I give him my grief over my father's death. I trust him with my failures and mistakes. I ask him to forgive my sins and transgressions.

And when I do, I "shall be comforted."

Here's the catch: we must give our mourning to God to receive his comfort. His word teaches: "Do not be anxious about anything, but in everything by prayer and supplication with thanksgiving let your requests be made known to God. And the peace of God, which surpasses all

25

understanding, will guard your hearts and your minds in Christ Jesus" (Philippians 4:6–7).

Have you done this?

Have you named your grief, your failure, your sin, and made him the king of it?

Have you put it in his hands and left it there?

If you will, God *will* comfort you. His Spirit will speak to your spirit, giving you the "peace of God." He will work through circumstances to bring you strength and help. His word will give you guidance and hope. He will lead people to bring you his wisdom and presence.

I don't know all the ways God will comfort you when you give him your mourning, but I promise you that he will. Scripture confirms his comfort:

- "Even though I walk through the valley of the shadow of death, I will fear no evil, for you are with me; your rod and your staff, they comfort me" (Psalm 23:4).

- "Sing for joy, O heavens, and exult, O earth; break forth, O mountains, into singing! For the Lord has comforted his people and will have compassion on his afflicted" (Isaiah 49:13).

- "The Lord is near to the brokenhearted and saves the crushed in spirit" (Psalm 34:18).

- "Come to me, all who labor and are heavy laden, and I will give you rest. Take my yoke upon you, and learn from me, for I am gentle and lowly in heart, and you will find rest for your souls" (Matthew 11:28–29).

Dwight Moody was right: "God never made a promise that was too good to be true."

Look for ways to comfort others

Expect to mourn. Then, when you trust your mourning to God, expect to be comforted.

One last principle: look for ways to comfort others. One of the most significant ways God comforts us is by using us to help others. I believe that God redeems all he allows. One way he redeems our suffering is by using it to help us help other people who are suffering.

His word is clear: "Blessed be the God and Father of our Lord Jesus Christ, the Father of mercies and God of all comfort, who comforts us in all our affliction, so that we may be able to comfort those who are in any affliction, with the comfort with which we ourselves are comforted by God" (2 Corinthians 1:3–4).

When our oldest son was diagnosed with cancer, people who had dealt with cancer could help us as others could not. When you have faced tragedy and struggles, people who have been where you are were God's instruments of healing.

Now we are called to pay it forward, to help others as we were helped, to be wounded healers.

Ask God to guide you to someone who is going through what you've been through. Ask him to open your eyes and heart to people he wants you to serve. Ask him to redeem your mourning by using it to comfort someone who is mourning. Ask him to use your experience of grace as an example to your culture.

And know that he will.

27

Conclusion

A. B. Simpson noted, "You will have no test of faith that will not fit you to be a blessing if you are obedient to the Lord. I never had a trial but when I got out of the deep river, I found some poor pilgrim on the bank that I was able to help by that very experience."

Consider some culture-changing examples.

Augustine was one of the most unrighteous men of his generation. He drifted from mistress to mistress, satisfying every lust and desire he felt.

Here's how he later described his condition: "I was held fast, not in fetters clamped upon me by another, but by my own will, which had the strength of iron chains. The enemy held my will in his power and from it he had made a chain and shackled me. For my will was perverse and lust had grown from it, and when I gave in to lust habit was born, and when I did not resist the habit it became a necessity. These were the links which together formed what I have called my chain, and it held me fast in the duress of servitude."

His "chain" held him until the day he took up the Scriptures, read of God's salvation in Christ, confessed his sins, and gave his heart to Jesus. And Jesus made him the greatest theologian after Paul in all of Christian history.

Gordon MacDonald was a successful pastor when he engaged in an extramarital sexual act. Immediately, he confessed this sin to his wife and congregation and resigned from his pulpit and the ministry. He entered into a long process of counseling and accountability, with no plans ever to reenter the pulpit ministry.

Then a church asked him to consider their pastorate.

He said that he was too broken to come. They said, "We're broken people, too." And through them God restored the repentant, broken, mourning preacher to his ministry. And through his ministry, God showed the world that he can restore all who trust in him.

Corrie ten Boom's story is familiar to you, I hope. She and her family harbored Jews in their home in Holland. For this, the Nazis arrested their family. All but Corrie died during the Holocaust. Years later, she returned to Germany. In her best-seller, *The Hiding Place*, Corrie describes what came next:

> It was at a church service in Munich that I saw him, the former S. S. man who had stood guard at the shower door in the processing center at Ravensbruck. He was the first of our actual jailers that I had seen since that time. And suddenly it was all there—the roomful of mocking men, the heaps of clothing, [my sister] Betsie's pain-blanched face.
>
> He came up to me as the church was emptying, beaming and bowing. "How grateful I am for your message, *Fraulein,*" he said. "To think that, as you say, He has washed my sins away!"
>
> His hand was thrust out to shake mine. And I, who had preached so often . . . the need to forgive, kept my hand at my side.
>
> Even as the angry, vengeful thoughts boiled through me, I saw the sin of them. Jesus Christ had died for this man; was I going to ask for more? Lord Jesus, I prayed, forgive me and help me to forgive him.

I tried to smile, I struggled to raise my hand.
I could not. I felt nothing, not the slightest
spark of warmth or charity. And so again
I breathed a silent prayer. Jesus, I cannot
forgive him. Give me Your forgiveness.

As I took his hand the most incredible thing
happened. From my shoulder along my arm
and through my hand a current seemed to
pass from me to him, while into my heart
sprang a love for this stranger that almost
overwhelmed me.

And so I discovered that it is not on our
forgiveness any more than on our goodness
that the world's healing hinges, but on His.
When He tells us to love our enemies, He
gives, along with the command, the love
itself.

Now, the comfort to forgive your pain, the comfort in
mourning Jesus gave to Corrie, he offers to you. And to the
world through you.

The day after my father died, a friend from college named
Ricky Wilcox drove across Houston to stay with me. I don't
remember that he said anything at all. He was just there.
And I'll never forget his kindness and the presence of Jesus
I sensed in him.

I didn't see him again that semester, then I graduated from
school, got married, and moved on to seminary. I have not
seen him since. I don't know where Ricky is today.

But I know this: he was God's gift to me that day. I want to
pay that gift forward to you today.

Now it's your turn.

Discussion Questions

1. What losses have especially marked your life?
    What made them so significant for you?

2. When you think of a hurting person who needs your
    ministry, who comes to mind first? What will you
    do to serve this person today?

3. How is such ministry relevant to your public
    influence?

CHAPTER 3

SUBMIT TO THE LORD

*"Blessed are the meek,
for they shall inherit the earth."*
—Matthew 5:5

If you replaced all the parts of a car, would it still be
the same car? To get more personal: since human cells
regenerate approximately every seven years, if you're more
than seven years old, is your body still the same body?

Consider the statement "This sentence is false." If it is
true, then it must be false, which means that it's true. But it
cannot be true since it claims to be false.

From the logical to the practical: Do you understand how talking into the rectangle we call a cell phone connects you to people on the other side of the world? Or how that device can download the entire internet to your hand?

Do you know how WiFi actually works? Do you know why it's called "WiFi"? (It's not short for "wireless fidelity," though most people think it is.)

Living in a world as complex as ours is a humbling thing. And that's a good thing, actually. A. W. Tozer: "For the Christian, humility is absolutely indispensable. Without it there can be no self-knowledge, no repentance, no faith and no salvation." St. Augustine: "Do you wish to rise? Begin by descending. You plan a tower that will pierce the clouds? Lay first the foundation of humility."

C. S. Lewis adds: "A proud man is always looking down on things and people; and, of course, as long as you are looking down, you cannot see something that is above you."

To see the Someone who is above you, choose humility. Jesus said it this way: "Blessed are the meek, for they shall inherit the earth" (Matthew 5:5). As we will see, being meek is indispensable to becoming culture-changing Christians. Let's learn why.

Value humility as God does

"Meek" translates the Greek word *praus*. It has several hues within its spectrum of meaning, but it reduces to the idea of humility before God. Such humility is consistently enjoined by Scripture:

- "Humble yourselves, therefore, under the mighty hand of God so that at the proper time he may exalt you" (1 Peter 5:6).

- "When pride comes, then comes disgrace, but with the humble is wisdom" (Proverbs 11:2).

- "Humble yourselves before the Lord, and he will exalt you" (James 4:10).

- "Before destruction a man's heart is haughty, but humility comes before honor" (Proverbs 18:12).

- "Do nothing from rivalry or conceit, but in humility count others more significant than yourselves" (Philippians 2:3).

Jesus promised that such people will "inherit the earth," being blessed by God in every way—not just part of the earth, but all the blessing God might give. No conqueror has ever won what God promises here.

But we try. We try to inherit the earth through our performance, possessions, and perfectionism by trying harder to do more, have more, or be more. And so, genuine humility is hard for many of us.

Like many people I have known over the years, I am a performer by nature. It is my natural personality to want you to like me, to be impressed by me, to affirm me. Many of us are this way. We live in a performance-dominated culture, where we are rewarded for what we can produce. But it's hard to want to impress people and be humble at the same time. Performing makes biblical humility hard.

On the other hand, many of us also struggle with self-esteem issues, making the wrong kind of humility easy. Consider this profound statement by psychologist Paul Tournier:

> I believe there is a great illusion underlying
> both the despair of the weak and the unease
> of the strong—and the misfortune of both.
> This great illusion is the very notion that
> there are two kinds of human beings, the
> strong and the weak. The truth is that human
> beings are much more alike than they think
> … All … in fact, are weak. All are weak
> because they are afraid. They are afraid of
> being trampled underfoot. They are all afraid
> of the inner weakness being discovered.
> They all have secret faults; they all have a
> bad conscience on account of certain acts
> which they would like to keep covered up.
> They are all afraid of other men and of God,
> of themselves, of life, and of death.

Many of us feel badly about ourselves, leading to a self-punishing, demeaning kind of humility. A performance-centered society and low self-image both make biblical humility hard for us.

But listen to what Jesus said about such humility. He described himself as "gentle and humble in heart" (Matthew 11:29 NIV). He promised us, "Whoever humbles himself like this child is the greatest in the kingdom of heaven" (Matthew 18:4). He warned us, "Everyone who exalts himself will be humbled, and he who humbles himself will be exalted" (Luke 14:11). And he taught us, "Now that I, your Lord and Teacher, have washed your feet, you also should wash one another's feet. I have set you an example that you should do as I have done for you" (John 13:14–15 NIV). The blunt fact is that we cannot be "blessed" by God unless we value humility as he does.

See yourself as God sees you

But valuing humility doesn't mean we know how to experience it. Here's the second biblical step: see yourself as God sees you. Dr. Martyn Lloyd-Jones defines *praus* or "meek" as "a humble and gentle attitude to others which is determined by a true estimate of ourselves." To be "meek" or "humble," develop a "true estimate" of yourself. Learn to see yourself the way God does.

So, how does God see you? As a redeemed sinner. A person who sinned and fell short of his glory; a person whose sins cost his Son his life; a person worthy of eternity in hell. And also a person he loves so much he gave his Son to die in your place, to pay for your sins, to purchase your salvation. A sinner redeemed by his love.

A rabbi once said, "A man should carry two stones in his pocket. On one should be inscribed, 'I am but dust and ashes.' On the other, 'For my sake was the world created.'" Both inscriptions are true.

Imagine yourself a condemned criminal on death row, scheduled for execution. All appeals are exhausted; the final hour has come. You are strapped to the gurney and tubes are inserted in your arm. The doctor is just about to administer the lethal injection—then the phone rings. The governor of the state is coming over.

When he arrives, something unprecedented occurs. He does not pardon you. He insists that your sentence be carried out. But he then orders the guards to remove you from the table. He takes off his coat and lies on your gurney. He rolls up his sleeve and orders the doctor to connect your tubes to his arm. He receives your injection; he takes your punishment; he dies for you.

For the rest of your life you will be a ransomed sinner, a condemned criminal. But you will also be someone loved beyond words by someone of great standing, of enormous power, of the highest significance.

This is exactly who you are. When we see ourselves as God does, our twin problems with humility are solved. We are set free from performance anxiety, the intense drivenness to impress people with our value, because we are valued by the Lord of the universe. And we are set free from debilitating, demeaning, demoralizing humility because we are valued by that same Lord.

You are a person of indescribable worth, not because of who you are but because of whose you are. See yourself as God does and you'll be freed for genuine humility.

See others as God sees them

Value humility as God does and see yourself as God does. Now you're ready for the third step to biblical humility: see others as God sees them.

Greek scholar Fritz Rienecker has this definition for *praus*: "The humble and gentle attitude which expresses itself in a patient submissiveness to offense, free from malice and desire for revenge." To be "meek" is to "submit to offense" no matter how others have offended you.

To do this, we must see others as God sees them: as people of infinite worth, for they are the creation of God, and as sinners just like us, saved by God's grace as we are. To be humble before others, do not judge them as better or worse than you are. Choose to pardon them when they hurt you, for God has pardoned you. Release your anger, or need for revenge, or pain.

When we do this, we are free to be humble before every person we know—not just before those we judge to be superior to us or those who humble us with their abilities or success. But also before those we consider inferior to us, those we judge and criticize and condemn. When we see him as God does, we can be humble before the lowest sinner.

Consider two assertions: "Only God is in position to look down on anyone" and "Any experience that makes me feel superior to other people is not of the Lord." See others as God sees them and you'll be humble before every person you know.

See your gifts as God sees them

Here's the last step: see your gifts and abilities as God sees them.

James Montgomery Boice defines *praus* as strength under control. He illustrates the word this way: a powerful stallion, strong and fast, completely bridled and submitted to the control of its master. To be "meek" is not to depreciate the stallion's strength, speed, or abilities. It is to submit them to the control of their master.

How does God see your abilities? As his gifts, entrusted to you to be used for his glory.

It is not biblical humility to debase yourself. Neither can you be humble when you exalt yourself.

It is biblical humility to embrace and affirm the gifts, abilities, opportunities, education, and experiences God has given to you, and then use them to glorify your Lord. Develop them fully and engage them completely.

One of my mentors said to me, "The Holy Spirit has a strange affinity for the trained mind." Develop fully all that God has given to you. But yield it to the control of God and use it for the glory of God.

Mother Teresa, the tiny Albanian nun, became the world's most famous Christian next to Billy Graham. But her goal was just the opposite. From the time she first entered ministry, her life purpose never changed. In her words, she wished only to be "a tiny pencil in the hand of God." And what he wrote with her gifts changed the world.

Conclusion

Why must we be *praus* to be culture-changing Christians?

The fact is, you and I cannot convict, save, or sanctify others. We cannot heal a marriage or spiritually transform a family. Only the Spirit of God can do these things.

But he cannot do through us what we try to do for him. If we do not humbly admit our need of his guidance and power, we will not experience his guidance and power. If we do not yield ourselves to his control, he cannot control us (cf. Ephesians 5:18). If we do not ask him to make us culture-changing Christians, we cannot become culture-changing Christians.

Do you value humility today as Jesus does? Do you see yourself as he does—a redeemed sinner, loved for whose you are? Do you see others as he does—fellow sinners, equal in value with you as your sisters and brothers? Do you see your abilities as he does—gifts to be used in his will for his glory? Are you completely submitted to his purpose in his power for his glory?

Then you are *praus*, "meek." And you are "blessed."

Here is one of the finest faith commitments I know, from a Muslim who became a Christian and prayed: "O God, I am Mustafah the tailor and I work at the shop of Muhammad Ali. The whole day long I sit and pull the needle and the thread through the cloth. O God, you are the needle and I am the thread. I am attached to you and I follow you. When the thread tries to slip away from the needle it becomes tangled and must be cut so that it can be put back in the right place. O God help me to follow you wherever you may lead me. For I am really only Mustafah the tailor, and I work at the shop of Muhammad Ali on the great square."

Whose "thread" are you?

Discussion Questions

1. How does our culture define humility? How does Jesus?

2. Is it hard for you to love yourself as unconditionally as Jesus does? Why?

3. What gifts and abilities are especially relevant to your cultural influence? How will you submit them to Jesus today?

CHAPTER 4

VALUE INTEGRITY

*"Blessed are those who hunger and thirst
for righteousness,
for they shall be satisfied."*
—Matthew 5:6

I saw some interesting signs recently:

- On a plumber's truck: "We repair what your husband fixed."

- At an optometrist's office: "If you don't see what you're looking for, you've come to the right place."

- Outside a muffler shop: "No appointment necessary. We heard you coming."

- Seen at a café: "If our food, drinks, and service aren't up to your standards, please lower your standards."

We're talking about success in this chapter.

What drives you? What defines success for you? If you could be anything in the world, what would you be? What *should* you be?

Let's ask Jesus.

What do you want?

"Blessed are the ones hungering and thirsting," Jesus begins in the literal Greek. Our Lord assumes that we all hunger and thirst for something. He doesn't say, "Blessed are you *if* you hunger and thirst . . . ." He knows that we do. And of course, he's right.

In his day, people knew physical hunger and thirst every day. People died without food or water. Droughts weren't a nuisance for the lawn but a threat to life itself. Crop failures didn't mean debt but death. While our society has passed that place, we're no less hungry and thirsty for the things that matter to us. We're all driven by something.

Theologian Paul Tillich was right: we each have an "ultimate concern," something or someone that matters more than anything else to us. There's something in your life that means success and significance to you.

That could be:

- raising successful children

- becoming president of your company

- retiring at fifty-five

- publishing best-selling books

- getting into the right school

- making the right grades

- having the right friends

- becoming a famous artist or doctor or lawyer or scientist or singer or teacher

- being "happy"

What drives you? What should?

How can you be sure that when you climb to the top of the ladder, it's not leaning against the wrong wall?

What constitutes success with God?

What makes us "blessed" by God?

For what should we "hunger and thirst"?

What should you want?

"Hunger and thirst after righteousness," Jesus continues. The Greek word translated *righteousness* reduces to the idea of uprightness, of doing what is right. But there's more to the term.

First, there's an **internal** sense here—personal character and morality. Not just what you do, but who you are.

Dwight Moody said that your character is what you are in the dark. It's been said that what you are when no one is looking is what you are.

"Righteousness" here requires personal, intimate holiness—a person whose attitudes and motives are just. The word means to be the same thing in private that you are in public, to be godly in character in both places, every day.

One reason to value such righteousness is that what we are in the dark is usually exposed to the light.

We read daily of business leaders who lied about the bottom line, fabricated profits, misrepresented in shareholder reports, and have to "take the fifth." But there's no fifth amendment with God.

A friend once said to me, "Happiness depends on circumstances; blessedness depends on character."

Righteousness is first internal and second **horizontal**. It points to our actions with others. The word means to practice uprightness and justice with all we know.

Abigail Adams, wife of our second president, once wrote to her sister Elizabeth, "To be good, and do good, is the whole duty of man."

Such horizontal righteousness is vital to our society. Speaking about corporate dishonesty, President George W. Bush made this eloquent and perceptive statement: "All investment is an act of faith, and faith is earned by integrity. In the long run, there is no capitalism without conscience; there is no wealth without character."

Righteousness is internal, then horizontal. And it is **vertical** as well: being right with God.

We are to be righteous in the sense of keeping God's commandments, living by his word, fulfilling his will. And by confessing our sins when we commit them, being sure nothing is wrong between us and our Father, and walking close to him.

Jesus makes this the key to character, the attribute for which we must "hunger and thirst" each day, the pathway to "blessing." If you can be only one thing, be righteous.

Niccolò Paganini was in concert with a full orchestra when a string snapped. He continued, improvising his solo. But a second string snapped, then a third. Three limp strings hung from Paganini's violin. He finished the difficult piece with one string, then held up the violin and said to the crowd, "Paganini and one string!" Then he played an encore on that one string.

What should your "one string" be?

Jesus makes the answer clear.

How do we achieve righteousness?

So, here's the practical question: How do we achieve righteousness with ourselves, others, and God? How do we play our lives on this string?

First, we must want to be righteous.

Decide that you will be godly in character, actions, and faith if you are nothing else. Choose holiness above everything. Hunger and thirst for it.

Settle for nothing less than righteousness as the central attribute of your character. Seek it with desperation and passion. Then you can receive it from God: "They will be filled," satisfied completely. If you hunger to be righteous, your hunger will be satisfied. But you must hunger first. You must want this food before you can have it.

Second, admit that you are not righteous without God.

Here's what God says of us: "There is no one righteous, not even one; there is no one who understands, there is no one who seeks God" (Romans 3:10–11 NIV). This is the biblical doctrine called "total depravity." It means that every part of our lives is affected by sin.

The cancer has metastasized throughout the body of the patient. The patient can still read the paper, drink coffee, even go to work perhaps; but the disease is everywhere, and death is inevitable.

In the eyes of a holy God, "there is no one righteous." Think about your last sin. That one sin alone is enough to keep you out of God's perfect heaven. So, admit that you cannot be righteous without the help of God.

Third, seek the righteousness of God by faith.

You cannot make yourself righteous. That's why Jesus' beatitude is in the passive tense: "They will be filled." Not "they will fill themselves," for we cannot. This is not a call to try harder to be better. It is not works righteousness. We can do better for a while, but, ultimately, we'll fall and fail again. I've tried. So have you.

Instead, accept this fact: "God made him who had no sin to be sin for us, so that in him we might become the righteousness of God" (2 Corinthians 5:21 NIV).

Christ is our righteousness. He will impart to us his Spirit, his holiness, and his character. This is the exchanged life. Believe that Christ lives in your heart, by faith. Ask him to make himself real through your character, your personality. Ask him to help you exhibit the righteousness of God.

Give him time to do so. Meet him in Scripture so he can transform your mind. Meet him in prayer so he can transform your spirit. Meet him in worship so he can transform your soul. Let the carpenter work with the wood, molding and shaping it into his own image. And believe that he is.

So, where do you need to be righteous today? Where are you grappling with sin or temptation—with yourself, with others, with God? Identify that issue right now.

Hunger and thirst for the righteousness of God.

Admit to him that you cannot make yourself righteous.

Be sure you've made Christ your Savior and Lord.

Ask him for his character, his holiness, his power, and his righteousness.

Spend time with him, allowing him to transform you into his image.

And you will be "blessed" indeed.

Conclusion

Our culture says good enough is good enough. So long as you're as moral as the rest of us, you're as moral as you need to be. Don't stand out—don't be different. Go along to get along.

Jesus says that if you want to live your best life, you must hunger and thirst for the righteousness only God can give. You must settle for nothing less than his character and his integrity, his Spirit powerfully working in and through your life. You must seek to be so much like Jesus that others see Jesus in you.

Why is such righteousness essential for culture-changing Christians? We cannot give what we do not have or lead where we will not go. If others do not see a difference in us, why would they want what we have?

Conversely, the more our culture morally deteriorates, the more obvious our character becomes. The darker the room, the brighter the light.

To change the culture, we must be "poor in spirit," asking the Holy Spirit to control our lives daily. Then we must mourn for our sins and failures, asking God to transform us and make us an example to others. We must be "meek," submitting every day to his Spirit's transformational leading and use.

And we must ask God to make us examples of what we are inviting others to experience. We must be the change we wish to see in others.

Are these imperatives your commitments today?

A group of American ministers once visited England to hear some of her famous preachers. On a Sunday morning, they attended the renowned City Temple. Some two thousand people filled the building, and the pastor's forceful personality dominated the service. His voice was powerful, his message biblical, and the Americans left saying, "What a wonderful preacher is [name]!"

That night, they heard Charles Spurgeon at the Metropolitan Tabernacle. The building was much larger and the congregation more than twice the size. Spurgeon's voice and oratory were the finest they had ever heard.

But the Americans soon forgot all about the building, the congregation, and the voice. They even overlooked their intention to compare the two preachers. When the service was over, they found themselves saying only, "What a wonderful Savior is Jesus Christ!"

What will people say about you this week?

Discussion Questions

1. What is your "ultimate concern" today? What
   should it be?

2. How does our culture make it difficult to live with
   godly integrity?

3. How is your personal character relevant to your
   public influence?

CHAPTER 5

CHOOSE TO PARDON

"Blessed are the merciful,
for they shall receive mercy."
—Matthew 5:7

There was some strange news as I wrote this chapter:

- A man built a pyramid from 1,030,315 pennies, setting a Guinness record. It took him three years.

- A man in Spain sold a block of blue cheese for $16,142.41.

- Another man fit 146 blueberries in his mouth, setting a Guinness record.

- And veterinarians removed nineteen pacifiers from the stomach of a bulldog named Mortimer. Following surgery, Mortimer is fully recovered.

Much of what makes headlines this week will be forgotten next week. If you want to do something unforgettable and life-changing, put today's beatitude into practice in your life.

Jesus declared: "Blessed are the merciful, for they shall receive mercy" (Matthew 5:7). Giving and receiving mercy leads to blessing we will never forget, on earth or in heaven.

Who is the person who has hurt you most deeply or recently? Who is the person you think of first when I ask you for someone you need to forgive?

Let's ask Jesus to help us do just that.

What is mercy?

Let's begin with the question: What is "mercy"?

Here's the short answer: grace is getting what you don't deserve; mercy is not getting what you do deserve. It's mercy to be forgiven. It's mercy to forgive. That's what mercy is.

Now, what is mercy *not*?

Ethicist Lewis Smedes offered these answers:

- Forgiving is not forgetting. God can forgive our confessed sins and forget them. In fact, he does: when we confess our sins to him, he promises that he "remembers your sins no more" (Isaiah 43:25 NIV). But you and I cannot do this. Human beings cannot simply reformat the disk or erase the tape. You can pull the nail out of your soul, but the hole remains

- Forgiving is not excusing the behavior that hurt you. The person chose to do that which hurts you today.

- Forgiving is not pretending you're not hurt. You can carry on, but the pain remains and often grows.

- Forgiving is not tolerating. You may have to tolerate your employer, or your sibling, or your son-in-law. That doesn't mean you've forgiven him.

To forgive is to pardon. It is to refuse to punish, even though you have every right to do so.

It is the governor pardoning the criminal: he doesn't forget about the crime, excuse it, pretend it didn't occur, or tolerate the behavior. He simply chooses not to punish, though he could.

So, who needs your pardon today?

As Smedes observes, you may need to pardon a parent who died and left you. The birth mother who gave you away. The "invisible ghost" in the organization who fired you, or mismanaged your investments, or cut your son from the squad or your daughter from the drill team. Someone who appears not to care if you forgive them or not.

Maybe God. Maybe yourself.

Why should you be merciful?

Why issue such a pardon?

First, to stop your personal cycle of pain.

This beatitude promises that the merciful will be "blessed" by God. This "blessing" transcends your pain. God offers you a ticket off the roller coaster of hurt.

But you must extend mercy to receive it.

If you give back what others give to you, you are constantly their victim. They pitch; you catch. You're trapped by your circumstances. Your soul is a genie in their bottle. How they rub it determines who you are.

If you refuse to pardon the person who hurt you, he hurts you still. Every time you plot your revenge, you feel your pain again. Every time you nurse your pain, you increase it.

The person who hurt you may not even know you're harboring your grudge and wounding your soul. He or she may have gone on with life. You're hurting no one more than yourself. But you can stop today.

Frederick Buechner: "Of the Seven Deadly Sins, anger is possibly the most fun. To lick your wounds, to smack your lips over grievances long past, to roll over your tongue the prospect of bitter confrontations still to come, to savor to the last toothsome morsel both the pain you are given and the pain you are giving back—in many ways it is a feast fit for a king. The chief drawback is that what you are wolfing down is yourself. The skeleton at the feast in you."

The second reason follows the first: pardon to receive mercy.

Jesus promises the merciful that "they will be shown mercy." This is not a transaction, a legal arrangement, as though my mercy obligates you and God to be merciful to me. Mercy is not a means to your end, but a free gift you choose to give.

But when you give it, a miraculous thing happens: You put yourself in position to receive mercy from God and others. Not because you earned it, but simply because now you're willing to receive it.

People who are the most legalistic with others are usually legalistic with themselves. If I won't forgive you until you're punished, I won't forgive myself until I'm punished. If I won't show mercy to you, I won't receive it myself.

I was once hurt by a deacon and his family in a church I pastored. The pain was real and deep. Every time I saw him in worship, I felt my anger well up in my soul. I became short, irritated, on edge with others—and especially with myself. Intolerant of my own mistakes and failures.

But the day I released my anger and chose to pardon that man, I found a new freedom with myself and a new willingness to be loved and forgiven by God.

If life must be fair and every injustice punished, we cannot forgive others—or ourselves.

Here's a third reason: pardon to break the circle of revenge.

If I must return your hurt, then you must return mine. And I must return yours. It has been truly said: You can no more win a war than win a fire.

But when you pardon me, the cycle stops. There's nothing left for me to do but to receive or reject your pardon. I have no cause to hurt you and abundant reason to love you and learn to love myself as well.

Here's a fourth reason: to show others the love of Christ.

Jesus identified one characteristic as a guarantee that others will know we love him: "By this all people will know you are my disciples, if you have love one for another" (John 13:35). Forgiving, pardoning, and releasing love proves that God's love in us is real.

During the depths of the Cold War, people in a particular East German town began throwing their trash over the Berlin Wall into the West German town on the other side. The West Germans, for their part, responded by tossing food and clothes to the East Germans—with this note: "Each gives what he has."

How can you be merciful?

Let's turn now to the practical question I hope you're now asking: How can you be merciful? How can you do as Jesus teaches here so that you stop your pain, experience mercy, break the cycle of revenge, and show others his love?

What practical steps can you take to offer mercy to the person who most needs it from you?

First, admit the reality of your hurt.

Name it honestly and specifically. Describe in words how you feel about it and the person who caused it. Describe even what you would like to do in revenge. Get your feelings out, as openly and transparently as possible.

You may want to put them on paper. Write a letter to the one who hurt you, then tear it up. You may want to talk to a friend you trust or a Christian counselor. Most of all, admit it to God. As someone said, "Tell God on them." Pour out your pain and hurt. You must admit the cancer exists before the surgeon can help you.

Second, ask God to help you pardon the one who hurt you.

You are not expected to be "merciful" without Jesus' help. That's why these Beatitudes are addressed to believers, followers of Christ. And why they are sequential. If we admit our need of God and mourn for our own sins, living under the control of the Spirit and seeking to be righteous in every relationship, then we can be empowered to extend to others the mercy we have received.

Turn to the Holy Spirit who dwells in your heart and soul. Ask him for the power and pardon of God. Ask him for the ability to see this person as he does. And to see yourself as he does—both of you redeemed sinners. Ask him to help you give to your enemy the mercy God has given to you.

And act as though he has. Don't feel yourself into a new way of acting; act yourself into a new way of feeling. Step out by faith. Every time the pain wells up inside your heart again, tell yourself that you have released this person from the prison of their sin. The ink on the pardon is dry, the deed is done, the forgiveness made.

Third, initiate restoration.

With God's help, act in courage. Jesus taught us to go directly to the person who sins against us (Matthew 18:15). Tell the person honestly what they did to you and how much this pain has hurt you. They may not even know their injustice or comprehend its severity. If I hurt you, I want to know it. I want you to talk to me, not about me. And I to you. Go to the person in question, with honesty.

Tell this person that you have pardoned him. He may not understand what you mean, or believe it, or accept it. She may never reciprocate what you have done. This is not yours to decide. You must begin the process of healing the relationship, whatever your partner in restoration decides to do.

And find an honest way to a new relationship. To forgive is not to be naïve. It is not to allow an unrepentant, unchanged person to hurt you yet again. Neither is it to assume that they will never change. Seek a wise balance with the wisdom God gives to know what and where you can trust. You may never have the old relationship, but you can have a new one by the mercy of God.

Last, be realistic.

We humans forgive slowly, a little at a time, usually with anger left over. Remind yourself that you have forgiven as many times as the pain comes back. Over time, it will come back less. And, one day, perhaps not at all.

Conclusion

To forgive, you must first be forgiven. You cannot give what you have never received.

Have you asked Jesus to forgive your sins, to pardon your failures, to be your Savior and Lord? He's waiting to do just that for you, right now. And to help you give his forgiveness to the person most in need of this gift from you.

Why is such forgiveness essential for culture-changing Christians?

If we will not forgive those who hurt us, how can we expect them to believe that God will forgive them? Conversely, if we offer them pardon in grace, we show that such grace from God is possible as well.

When the great astronomer Copernicus lay dying, a copy of his magnum opus, *The Revolution of the Heavenly Bodies*, was placed in his hands. But he was not thinking of his brilliant scientific discoveries or the universal acclaim they won him. His mind was on a far higher plane.

As one of his last acts, he directed that this epitaph be placed on his grave: "O Lord, the faith thou didst give to St. Paul, I cannot ask; the mercy thou didst show to St. Peter,

I dare not ask; but Lord, the grace thou didst show unto the dying robber, that, Lord, show to me."

Every person can come to God under these terms. And every person can give them to others. Even us. Even now.

Take a little quiz with me: Name the wealthiest person in the world. Name the last two Heisman Trophy winners, or the last winner of the Miss America pageant, or the last recipient of the Nobel Peace Prize.

When you truly forgive someone for what they did to you, you will never forget it. Neither will they. And your culture will take note, to the glory of God.

Discussion Questions

1. When you envision those who have hurt you, what person comes to mind first? What is the most challenging aspect of pardoning this person?

2. Would you ask God to help you offer forgiveness? Would you ask him to lead your next step toward restoration and reconciliation?

3. How is pardoning others significant for your public witness?

CHAPTER 6

LOVE GOD AND PEOPLE

*"**Blessed are the pure in heart,
for they shall see God.**"*
—Matthew 5:8

*There are three tame ducks in our back yard,
Dabbling in mud and trying hard
To get their share, and maybe more,
Of the overflowing barnyard store.*

*Satisfied with the task they're at,
Eating and sleeping and getting fat.*

But whenever the free wild ducks go by
In a long line streaming down the sky,
They cock a quizzical, puzzled eye,
And flap their wings and try to fly.

I think my soul is a tame old duck,
Dabbling around in barnyard muck,
Fat and lazy with useless wings.

But sometimes when the North wind sings
And the wild ones hurdle overhead,
It remembers something lost and dead,
And cocks a wary, bewildered eye,
And makes a feeble attempt to fly.

It's fairly content with the state it's in,
But it isn't the duck it might have been.

I don't want to be a tame duck. You don't, either. You want your life to have purpose and passion, a reason for being that transcends the humdrum routine, the workaday world. You want to believe that your life counts for something bigger than yourself, that you are more than a dot on the screen of the universe.

How do we escape the barnyard? And why is a life of purpose essential to changing our culture for the glory of God?

Choose to have a life purpose

"Blessed are the pure in heart, for they shall see God," Jesus assures us.

Greek scholar Fritz Rienecker defines "heart" as "the center of the inner life of the person where all the spiritual forces and functions have their origin."

Here, "pure" means to have integrity, to be consistent, to be of one mind.

So, to be "pure in heart" is to have a single purpose to your life. Kierkegaard was right: "purity of heart is to will one thing"—to choose to have a single life purpose.

Not everyone believes you can. Many believe that life has no real purpose or meaning.

Philosopher Martin Heidegger says you're an actor on a stage with no script, director, audience, past or future. Courage is to face life as it is.

"Postmodernism" says there's no absolute truth, which is itself an absolute truth claim. Life has no real purpose, just what you make of it. Life is chaotic, random dots produced by the coincidence of evolution and the chance occurrences of life.

Why not share this chaotic worldview? Why seek to be "pure of heart," to have a single purpose?

One answer is practical.

Greatness is only possible through commitment to a single purpose.

Winston Churchill in June of 1941: "I have only one purpose, the destruction of Hitler, and my life is much simplified thereby." Brilliant scholar and author William Barclay: "A man will never become outstandingly good at anything unless that thing is his ruling passion. There must be something of which he can say, 'For me to live is this.'"

A second answer is logical.

If the universe were chaotic, without purpose or meaning, you and I would never be able to know it or say it.

Think with me for a moment. If reality were truly chaotic, there would be nothing we could "know." Red today would be green tomorrow. Stand before a Jackson Pollock painting, splotches on the canvas, and tell me what it "means." Or before a Mark Rothko, a canvas painted all a single solid color. Again, there is no intrinsic meaning.

If the world were chaos like their paintings, there could be no objective truth, not even the objective statement that there is no objective truth. And we couldn't speak of truth, for language could have no common meaning between us.

A third answer is biblical.

Jesus made this statement about human experience: "No one can serve two masters, for either he will hate the one and love the other, or he will be devoted to the one and despise the other" (Matthew 6:24).

James added this command: "Cleanse your hands, you sinners, and purify your hearts, you double-minded" (James 4:8). To purify our heart, we must not be "double-minded." We must have a single life purpose.

A fourth answer is spiritual.

We must be "pure in heart" to see God. Jesus' beatitude makes this fact clear.

We cannot see God with our physical eyes: "You cannot see my face, for man shall not see me and live" (Exodus 33:20). But we can "see" God spiritually. Hebrews 11:27 says of Moses, "he endured as seeing him who is invisible." Exodus 33:11 states, "The Lord used to speak to Moses face to face, as a man speaks to his friend."

We can know God this intimately. But only if we are pure in heart: "Without holiness no one will see the Lord"

(Hebrews 12:14 NIV). But Jesus promises: if we are "pure in heart," we will.

Choose the right life purpose

So, how do we become "pure in heart"?

Assuming that these practical, logical, biblical, and spiritual arguments are compelling, what do you do next? What single life purpose will lead us to "see God"?

We're not the first to ask Jesus.

Remember the lawyer's trick question: "Teacher, which is the greatest commandment in the Law?" (Matthew 22:36 NIV). In other words, which of our 613 commandments will you neglect so we can convict you of breaking the law?

And remember Jesus' answer, summarizing all the law and the prophets, all the word and will of God: "Love the Lord your God with all your heart and with all your soul and with all your mind . . . . love your neighbor as yourself" (vv. 37, 39).

The two are one in Jesus' answer to the lawyer's request for the greatest single commandment in God's word. They are two wings of the same spiritual airplane, both essential for the soul that flies into the presence of God. Examine them for a moment.

Love the Lord "with all your heart," by walking in the will of God.

Remember that your heart is the center of your life, the origin of your will and actions. The Bible instructs us, "Flee the evil desires of youth, and pursue righteousness, faith, love and peace, along with those who call on the Lord out of a pure heart" (2 Timothy 2:22 NIV). Flee evil, pursue righteousness. Walk in the will of God and you'll be "pure in heart."

67

Love the Lord "with all your soul," by practicing the worship of God.

Love the Lord with your spiritual life, your daily worship: "Give me an undivided heart, that I may fear your name" (Psalm 86:11 NIV). To "fear" God is to reverence him, to honor him, to worship him. The "undivided heart" is the pure heart. Love God with your daily worship, as you commune with him, walk with him, praise him. And you'll be "pure in heart."

Love the Lord "with all your mind," by knowing the word of God.

Know and obey his revealed truth: "Having purified your souls by your obedience to the truth . . ." (1 Peter 1:22). Know and obey the truth of God's word and you'll be "pure in heart."

And love the world as God does.

"The aim of our charge is love that issues from a pure heart" (1 Timothy 1:5).

Share God's love by living your faith. As Francis of Assisi purportedly suggested, preach the gospel at all times; when necessary, use words. Share God's love by caring for hurting souls. Show them God's love in yours. Share God's love by explaining your faith. Share with them God's salvation and urge them to experience his grace.

And you'll be "pure in heart."

Conclusion

If you and I have the singular purpose of loving our Lord and loving our neighbor, such a radical passion and compassion will impact those we influence. They will see in us a joy they will want for themselves. They will find in us a simplicity and sincerity of life that will challenge and encourage them. In short, they will want to love our Lord if we love him and we love them.

A crash once closed a road leading to the Denver International Airport. Google Maps offered drivers a quick way out of the traffic jam. However, the route it suggested took them down a dirt road that rain had turned into a muddy mess. Some vehicles couldn't drive through the mud and became stuck. About a hundred others became trapped behind them.

They were sincere in trusting the app, but they were sincerely wrong.

This beatitude offers us the only path to a life God can bless. So, choose to have a single life purpose, for practical, logical, biblical, and spiritual reasons. Choose Jesus' purpose: love the Lord your God with your heart through his worship, with your soul through his will, and with your mind through his word. Love others as yourself and you will be "pure in heart."

And you will see God.

Your soul can be a tame duck. Or it can be a wild eagle.

The choice is yours.

Discussion Questions

1. Finish the sentence: My ministry is
   _____.

2. In what ways does our culture make it difficult to love God and others?

3. How is such a life purpose relevant to your public influence?

CHAPTER 7

SEEK PEACE

*"Blessed are the peacemakers,
for they shall be called sons of God."*
—Matthew 5:9

A friend sent me these first-grade proverbs. The teacher gave the kids the first half of the sentence, and they supplied the rest:

- "Don't bite the hand that . . . looks dirty."

- "If you lie down with dogs, you'll . . . stink in the morning."

- "A penny saved is . . . not much."

- "Laugh and the whole world laughs with you, cry and . . . you have to blow your nose."

- "Better to be safe than . . . punch a fifth grader."

Even first-graders know that peace is valuable. And they're right. It has been estimated that in the last 3,400 years, humans have been entirely at peace for 268 of them, constituting 8 percent of recorded history.

Clearly, our world needs peace. Where do you? With whom are you at odds today? Where do you need a relationship to be healed? Where do you need peace?

"Blessed are the peacemakers, for they will be called sons of God," Jesus promises. The Hebrew word for peace is *shalom*: peace with God, self and others. Let us now learn from God's word where we find such peace for ourselves, and then how we can give it to the person with whom we need it most.

Make peace with God

Where can you find peace for your own heart, soul, and mind?

The Bible says, "May the Lord give strength to his people! May the Lord bless his people with peace!" (Psalm 29:11).

Jesus promised us, "Peace I leave with you; my peace I give to you. Not as the world gives do I give to you. Let not your hearts be troubled, neither let them be afraid" (John 14:27). Later he said, "I have said these things to you that in me you may have peace. In the world you will have tribulation. But take heart; I have overcome the world." (John 16:33).

Peace is one of the "fruit of the Spirit" (Galatians 5:22). It is the result of the Spirit's work, not human ability.

Clearly, we cannot create peace ourselves. We can only receive it from God. How? Here are some answers from God's word.

First, if you want peace, accept the love of God.

Actress Sophia Loren told *USA Today*, "I should go to heaven; otherwise it's not nice. I haven't done anything wrong. My conscience is very clean. My soul is as white as those orchids over there, and I should go straight, straight to heaven."

Listen, by contrast, to the word of God.

- The prophet said of Jesus, "But he was pierced for our transgressions; he was crushed for our iniquities; upon him was the chastisement that brought us peace, and with his wounds we are healed." (Isaiah 53:5).

- Paul added, "For he himself is our peace, who has made us both one and has broken down in his flesh the dividing wall of hostility" (Ephesians 2:14).

- When we accept Jesus' forgiving love by faith, we receive God's peace: "Therefore since we have been justified by faith, we have peace with God through our Lord Jesus Christ." (Romans 5:1).

We cannot be at peace with a perfect God and live in his perfect heaven unless we are made perfect ourselves. This is why Jesus died on the cross: to pay the penalty for our sins, to purchase our forgiveness. We can only be at peace with God by accepting his love, by making Jesus our Savior and Lord.

If you're trying to be good enough for God—religious enough, moral enough, successful or significant enough—know that you're not succeeding. Imagine what it would take for a human being to impress the God of the universe. But we can accept the atoning love of Jesus and be made right with God. This is the first step to true peace.

Next, obey the word of God.

Musician Paul Simon once told an interviewer, "The only thing that God requires from us is to enjoy life—and love. It doesn't matter if you accomplish anything. You don't have to do anything but appreciate that you're alive. And love, that's the whole point."

Note the contrast between his statement and God's word.

The Psalmist prayed, "Great peace have those who love your law; nothing can make them stumble" (Psalm 119:165). God said through his prophet, "Oh that you had paid attention to my commandments! Then your peace would have been like a river, and your righteousness like the waves of the sea" (Isaiah 48:18).

God's word gives the guideposts we need to live successfully. Here are the signs that point us to our destination and keep us out of ditches and dead ends. These principles are for our good, and they give us God's peace.

So, meet God every day in the Scriptures. Measure your every decision by his truth. Obey his word, and you'll have his peace.

Third, receive the forgiveness of God.

Dwight Moody gave a Bible to a friend but first wrote these words on its flyleaf: "The Bible will keep you from sin, or sin will keep you from the Bible."

When we obey the word of God, we judge ourselves in its light. We see ourselves as God does. The closer we are to God, the further away we realize we are. Then we seek and receive his forgiveness for our sins, and we have his peace.

God told the prophet, "There is no peace for the wicked" (Isaiah 48:22). He added: "But the wicked are like the tossing sea, which cannot rest, whose waves cast up mire and mud" (Isaiah 57:20 NIV). And he warned: "The way of peace they do not know, and there is no justice in their paths; they have made their roads crooked; no one who treads on them knows peace" (Isaiah 59:8).

His word is clear: "Be sure your sin will find you out" (Numbers 32:23). So, confess your sins to God if you want to have peace with him. He is waiting to forgive you, cleanse you, and set you free. He loves you that much. But you must ask.

Fourth, trust the will of God.

Advice from the Book of Job: "Agree with God, and be at peace; thereby good will come to you." (Job 22:21). Paul agreed: "And let the peace of Christ rule in your hearts, to which indeed you were called in one body. And be thankful." (Colossians 3:15).

Trust the will of God and you'll say with the prophet: "You keep him in perfect peace whose mind is stayed on you, because he trusts in you." (Isaiah 26:3). Are you at peace with God today? Have you accepted his love? Are you obeying his word? Have you received his forgiveness? Are you trusting his will?

H. G. Wells was right: "If there is no God, nothing matters. If there is a God, nothing else matters." God promises you his peace and tells you how to receive it. The decision is yours.

Make peace with others

Now, how do we give this peace we receive from God? How do we become "peacemakers" with others? With whom do you most need peace today? Think of that person and take these biblical steps toward the peace you need.

First, initiate pardon.

As we learned from the fifth beatitude, we are to choose not to punish whatever wrong has been done to us. God's word instructs us, "If possible, so far as it depends on you, live peaceably with all. Beloved, never avenge yourselves, but leave it to the wrath of God, for it is written, 'Vengeance is mine, I will repay,' says the Lord" (Romans 12:18–19).

Later, the apostle adds, "Do not be overcome by evil, but overcome evil with good" (Romans 12:21). Initiate pardon and you will be a peacemaker.

Second, seek reconciliation.

Jesus teaches us, "So if you are offering your gift at the altar and there remember that *your brother has something against you*, leave your gift there before the altar and go. First be reconciled to your brother, and then come and offer your gift" (Matthew 5:23–24, emphasis added).

If someone has something against you, whether you believe their anger is justified or not, go to them. Seek reconciliation and you will be a peacemaker.

Third, choose peace.

Whether the person accepts your pardon or receives your attempts at reconciliation, choose peace. Give them to God and choose his peace.

The Bible says, "God has called you to peace" (1 Corinthians 7:15). It exhorts us: "Be at peace among yourselves (1 Thessalonians 5:13). Our Master tells us, "Welcome one another as Christ has welcomed you" (Romans 15:7).

God commands us: "Strive for peace with everyone, and for the holiness without which no one will see the Lord. See to it that no one fails to obtain the grace of God; that no 'root of bitterness' springs up and causes trouble, and by it many become defiled" (Hebrews 12:14–15).

When we have God's peace in our heart, we can give it to others. And when we give peace to others, we find it in our own heart. As we love God, we love our neighbor. As we love our neighbor, we love God.

And then we "will be called sons of God." Jesus does not say that we *become* sons of God—that would be works righteousness. But people will know that we are God's children as we give his peace to them: "By this all people will know that you are my disciples, if you have love for one another" (John 13:35).

Conclusion

Is your soul at peace with those who matter to you? Would you seek peace with God and with them?

Why is being at peace with God and others essential to becoming culture-changing Christians? Because a world of conflict and chaos will always take note of people who are at peace.

Consider John Wesley, the founder of Methodism and one of the most significant Christian leaders in history. He went to America as a missionary but was not himself converted.

He wrote in his journal, "I went to America to convert the Indians, but oh! who shall convert me?"

Then he encountered Moravian missionaries on board a ship bound for America. He notes in his journal that, one day, the group had just begun to sing a psalm of worship when "the sea broke over, split the mail-sail in pieces, covered the ship, and poured in between the decks, as if the great deep had already swallowed us up. A terrible screaming began among the English. The Germans [Moravians] calmly sung on. I asked one of them afterwards, 'Was you not afraid?' He answered, 'I thank God, No.' I asked, 'But were not your women and children afraid?' He replied mildly, 'No; our women and children are not afraid to die.'

"From them I went to their crying, trembling neighbours, and pointed out to them the difference in the hour of trial, between him that feareth God, and him that feareth him not. At twelve the wind fell. This was the most glorious Day which I have hitherto seen."

Wesley later testified that the Moravians' peace contributed directly to his conversion.

Who will see the peace of Christ in you?

Francis of Assisi was riding on horseback down the road that went by a leper colony far from his home. He had recently sensed God leading him into a life of spiritual service, but he was still caught by the lure of wealth and glory.

Historian Arnaldo Fortini picks up the story: "Suddenly the horse jerked to the side of the road. With difficulty Francis pulled him back by a violent jerk at the reins. The young man looked up and recoiled in horror. A leper stood in the middle of the road, a short distance away, unmoving, and looking at him. He was no different from the others, the usual wan specter, with stained face, shaved head, dressed in gray sackcloth. He did not speak and showed no sign of moving, of getting out of the way. He looked at the horseman fixedly, strangely, with an acute and penetrating gaze.

"An instant that seemed eternity passed. Slowly Francis dismounted, went to the man, took his hand. It was a cold emaciated hand, bloodstained, twisted, inert and cold like that of a corpse. He put a mite of charity in it, pressed it, carried it to his lips. And suddenly, as he kissed the lacerated flesh of the creature who was the most abject, the most hated, the most scorned, of all human beings, he was flooded with a wave of emotion, one that shut out everything around him, one that he would remember even on his death bed.

"As the leper withdrew his hand, Francis raised his head to look at him again. He was no longer there."

When young Francis of Assisi gave a hurting soul the peace of God, he found it in his own heart.

So will we.

Discussion Questions

1. In what ways is it challenging to live at peace with God, others, and yourself in our culture?

2. With whom do you need greater peace today? What steps will you take in response?

3. How is being at peace with God, others, and yourself important to your cultural influence?

CHAPTER 8

SERVE CHRIST WITH COURAGE

"Blessed are those who are persecuted
for righteousness' sake, for theirs is the
kingdom of heaven."
—Matthew 5:10

Christians are the most persecuted religious group in
the world, according to a recent report. The study cites
bombings of churches in Egypt, Pakistan, and Indonesia;
the torture of Christians in North Korean and Eritrean
prisons; social persecution in North Korea, Saudi Arabia,
China, and other countries; and attacks on Christian
minorities in India, China, and other nations.

According to Gary Bauer, a commissioner on the US Commission on International Religious Freedom (USCIRF), "Christians are the most persecuted religious group in the world and it's accelerating."

While 30 percent of the world's population identifies as Christian, 80 percent of all acts of religious discrimination around the world are directed at Christians. One scholar estimates that 90 percent of all people killed on the basis of their religious beliefs are Christians. The USCIRF has identified sixteen countries where "heinous and systematic" offenses, including torture, imprisonment, and murder, occur against religious communities. The only religion under attack in all sixteen countries is Christianity.

According to Jesus, we should not be surprised when we face opposition for our faith. Those who hate our Father will hate his children. This is just as true in America as it is anywhere else in the world. When atheist Sam Harris claims that "science must destroy religion," he speaks for many who claim that religion is not just irrelevant but dangerous.

How should we respond when we are attacked for our faith? How can God redeem such attacks by using them to help us change the culture today?

Expect persecution

Jesus' beatitude can be literally translated, "Blessed are the ones who have been and now are being persecuted for the sake of righteousness." He knew his followers would suffer for their commitment to him. And they did.

They were "reviled" (v. 11), the objects of gossip, slander, and ridicule. Enemies of Christ said "all kinds of evil" against them. Because they shared a meal that symbolized the body and blood of Christ, they were accused of cannibalism. Because they called this meal the "love feast" and welcomed prostitutes into their churches, they were accused of sexual perversion. Because they would not bow before a bust of the emperor and say "Caesar is Lord," they were accused of atheism and sedition.

Persecution was a daily fact of life for them.

Before he was crucified upside down, the apostle Peter wrote: "Beloved, do not be surprised at the fiery trial when it comes upon you to test you, as though something strange were happening to you. But rejoice insofar as you share Christ's sufferings, that you may also rejoice and be glad when his glory is revealed" (1 Peter 4:12–13).

Jesus warned his disciples, "When they persecute you in one town, flee to the next" (Matthew 10:23).

William Barclay:

> All the world knows of the Christians who were flung to the lions or burned at the stake; but these were kindly deaths. Nero wrapped the Christians in pitch and set them alight, and used them as living torches to light his gardens. He sewed them in the skins of wild animals and set his hunting dogs upon them to tear them to death. They were tortured on the rack; they were scraped with pincers; molten lead was poured hissing upon them; red hot brass plates were affixed to the tenderest parts of their bodies; eyes were torn out; parts of their bodies were cut off and roasted before their eyes; their hands and feet were burned while cold water was poured over them to lengthen the agony. These things

are not pleasant to think about, but these are the things a man had to be prepared for, if he took his stand with Christ.

Persecution has remained a fact accompanying the Christian faith across all the centuries from their day to ours.

Seventy million believers have been murdered across Christian history for no reason except that they would not renounce their faith in Jesus. More believers were martyred in the twentieth century than the previous nineteen combined.

Totalitarian regimes cannot tolerate our commitment to Christ as Lord. Secular culture does not understand our convictions.

And Satan hates us. Jesus called him "a murderer from the beginning" (John 8:44). Peter warned us: "Your adversary the devil prowls around like a roaring lion, seeking someone to devour" (1 Peter 5:8).

Six centuries ago, Thomas à Kempis observed, "The devil sleepeth not, neither is the flesh as yet dead, therefore cease not to prepare thyself for the battle, for on thy right hand and on thy left are enemies who never rest."

He is still right.

Evaluate your courage

If you're like most of us, you may be a bit uncomfortable right now. It is a biblical fact that Christians should experience persecution for their faith, but many of us reading these words do not.

People at school may make fun of us if they learn we are

believers. Coworkers or clients may shun us if we don't join in ungodly activities. We may lose money or status when we refuse dishonesty or immorality. But, by and large, American Christians live in communities that expect us to be nominally Christian. Nothing extreme or intolerant, of course. But religion in moderation is accepted and even welcomed.

So, I've asked myself a hard question: Why don't I face more suffering for my faith? If indeed my fallen world is opposed to my commitment to Christ, and if Satan is my mortal enemy, why doesn't my faith cost me more? In the spiritual battle being waged for the souls of humanity, why don't we suffer more?

Here are the reasons which seem clear to me.

One: Some of us have withdrawn from the battle.

Many of us don't know many non-Christians. We spend so much of our time in the huddle that we have little contact with the other team.

At one of my pastorates, our church was preparing for "Friend Day," a Sunday when each member would bring a guest. But the chairman of our deacons objected: "I don't know anyone who doesn't go to church." And the other deacons nodded in agreement.

We're no threat to Satan unless we get on his turf.

Two: Some of us look like the enemy.

Jesus called us the "salt of the earth" and "light of the world" (Matthew 5:13–16). But if we lose our "saltiness" or hide our candle, the world doesn't feel our salt sting or see our light shine.

We can be one person at church but another at school, at work, at home, or with friends. We can stand with a foot in both worlds. We can speak church language and world language. We can employ church ethics and world ethics. We can wear church masks and world masks.

When we look like the enemy, we cost Satan nothing. He'd rather leave us where we are.

Three: Some of us are not willing to take a risk.

Many of us are regularly engaged with nonbelievers, and we are willing for them to know of our faith. But only to a point.

Only if they won't be offended if we share Christ with them or invite them to church. Only if they won't think us strange for our spirituality. Only if we can still be included in the social group we value or still make the money we want or still achieve the social status to which we aspire.

We don't suffer in the battle because we won't go to the front lines.

Choose to risk

Here's the relevant question today: Why change?

What are those of us who don't risk anything for our faith missing?

Jesus' last beatitude tells us.

First, suffering believers experience great joy.

According to Jesus, those who suffer for their faith will be "blessed"—the word refers to joy transcending our circumstances. Jesus told risk-taking Christians to "rejoice." There is joy in facing persecution for Jesus.

He also told us to "be glad," words that translate a Greek term that means to leap much with irrepressible joy. He was right. There is great joy in suffering for Christ. The apostles felt it: "When [the authorities] had called in the apostles, they beat them and charged them not to speak in the name of Jesus and let them go. Then they left the presence of the council, rejoicing that they were counted worthy to suffer dishonor for the name" (Acts 5:40–41).

Early martyrs felt it. There is an ancient tradition that states that Nero would walk at night on the Coliseum floor, examining the bodies of slain Christians left there. And wherever a body had a face, the face was smiling. Justin, one of the earliest martyrs, wrote to his accusers: "You can kill us but you cannot hurt us."

Second, suffering believers receive a great reward.

Paul was sure of it: "For I consider that the sufferings of this present time are not worth comparing with the glory that is to be revealed to us" (Romans 8:18). Martyr Jim Elliott wrote in his journal: "He is no fool who gives what he cannot keep to gain what he cannot lose."

Revelation promises those who suffer for Christ: "They shall hunger no more, neither thirst anymore; the sun shall not strike them, nor any scorching heat. For the lamb in the midst of the throne will be their shepherd, and he will guide them to springs of living water, and God will wipe away every tear from their eyes" (Revelation 7:16–17).

Third, suffering believers join a great fraternity.

At the end of the beatitudes, Jesus said, "Rejoice and be glad, for your reward is great in heaven, *for so they persecuted the prophets who were before yo*u" (Matthew 5:12, emphasis added).

The book of Hebrews described those who suffered for serving the one true God: "Some were tortured, refusing to accept release, so that they might rise again to a better life. Others suffered mocking and flogging, and even chains and imprisonment. They were stoned, they were sawn in two, they were killed with the sword. They went about in skins of sheep and goats, destitute, afflicted, mistreated—of whom the world was not worthy—wandering about in deserts and mountains, and in dens and caves of the earth" (Hebrews 11:35–38).

Every disciple but John was martyred, and John was exiled and imprisoned. Seventy million Christians have died since for following Jesus. When we suffer for Christ, we join a great fraternity in the faith.

Last, suffering believers inherit a great kingdom.

"Theirs is the kingdom of heaven" (Matthew 5:10). The first beatitude made this promise; the last repeats it. When we suffer for Christ, we prove that he is our king. And then we join him in his kingdom.

Second Timothy 2:12 promises: "If we endure, we will also reign with him." Revelation 20 describes those who stood faithful to Christ in the face of extreme persecution: "They came to life and reigned with Christ" (v. 4).

We will suffer for a short while and then reign with Jesus in his kingdom forever.

Conclusion

Why is courage in facing persecution vital for culture-changing Christians?

One reason is that the more we seek to influence the culture for Christ, the more we can expect the culture to reject us and Satan to oppose us. When we move onto the enemy's turf, the enemy fights back.

A second reason is that when we suffer for Jesus, secular people take note of the sincerity of our faith. The *Epistle to Diognetus* (AD 130) described early believers: "They are evil spoken of and yet are justified; they are reviled, and bless; they are insulted, and repay the insult with honour; they do good, yet are punished as evil-doers. When punished, they rejoice as if quickened into life." Their willingness to suffer for Jesus greatly empowered their witness.

So, here's the question: Are you suffering for your faith today? Choose to be faithful, and you'll forever be grateful.

Conversely, are you refusing risk and suffering for your faith? It's not too late to be faithful to the One who is faithful to you.

Sundar Singh was one of India's most famous Christians. He lived from 1889 to 1929, enduring extreme persecution for his courageous faith.

His family tried to poison him when he became a Christian. He was stoned and arrested numerous times, roped to a tree as bait for wild animals, and sewn into a wet animal skin and left to be crushed to death as it shrank in the hot sun. He disappeared while on a missionary journey. Indian Christians consider him their Francis of Assisi.

Here's the statement by Sundar Singh that drew me to him: "From my many years' experience I can unhesitatingly say that the cross bears those who bear the cross."

Will you bear yours?

Discussion Questions

1. Are you facing cultural opposition for your faith today? Why or why not?

2. Will you ask God for the courage to be faithful to your Lord in every circumstance today?

3. How is such courage relevant to your public influence?

CHAPTER 9

CHANGED PEOPLE CHANGE THE WORLD

I preached my first sermon in the fall of 1976. If I could have somehow read a copy of today's *New York Times* or *Dallas Morning News*, I would have struggled to believe what I found.

By 1976, nearly four million babies had been killed following the Supreme Court's ruling in 1973 legalizing abortion. Today, the number in America exceeds sixty million.

That year, gay rights protesters took to the streets at the Democratic National Convention in New York City. Few watching their protests imagined that same-sex marriage would one day be the law of the land and those who affirm biblical sexual morality would face escalating opposition from the culture.

In 1976, the New Jersey Supreme Court decided the first "right to die" case, ruling that patients have the right to decline medical treatment. Today, one in five Americans has access to physician-assisted death.

When I preached my first sermon, who would have predicted that the American Psychological Association would one day launch a "Consensual Non-Monogamy Task Force" for the purpose of promoting "awareness and inclusivity about consensual non-monogamy" such as "polyamory, open relationships, swinging, [and] relationship anarchy"? Or that a movie about a sexual relationship between a man and a dolphin would win "Best Documentary Short Film" at the Los Angeles Film Festival?

Who would have predicted that the percentage of Americans with no religious affiliation would triple from 1976 to today? Or that those who describe themselves as Protestants would fall from 60 percent to 35 percent?

No matter which direction we turn, it is clear that our nation needs a transformative movement of culture-changing Christians. However, we must be what we wish others to become. We must model what we ask others to emulate.

So, what does a culture-changing Christian look like? What values and commitments define such followers of Jesus?

In studying our Lord's beatitudes, we have discovered eight priorities that define and empower us as the "salt and light" Jesus intends us to be.

To review what we've learned from Matthew 5:

1. "Blessed are the poor in spirit, for theirs is the kingdom of heaven" (v. 3): We begin every day by submitting to the Holy Spirit, seeking his empowering and leading through our life and service.

2. "Blessed are those who mourn, for they shall be comforted" (v. 4): We stand with those who suffer, showing God's love in our compassion.

3. "Blessed are the meek, for they shall inherit the earth" (v. 5): We submit daily to God's control, trusting him to use our gifts and opportunities to advance his kingdom.

4. "Blessed are those who hunger and thirst for righteousness, for they shall be satisfied" (v. 6): We seek to be people of personal integrity so the Spirit can use us and others will see Christ in us.

5. "Blessed are the merciful, for they shall receive mercy" (v. 7): As an example of God's grace, we choose to pardon those who have hurt us.

6. "Blessed are the pure in heart, for they shall see God" (v. 8): We live for the singular purpose of loving God and others with passion and joy.

7. "Blessed are the peacemakers, for they shall be called sons of God" (v. 9): We choose to be at peace with God, others, and ourselves so as to offer God's peace to our fallen world.

8. "Blessed are those who are persecuted for righteousness' sake, for theirs is the kingdom of heaven" (v. 10): We face the opposition of our culture with courage and joy.

Which of these values is God's call to you now?

The Chinese theologian Watchman Nee made an assertion that has marked my life since I first encountered it:

> A day must come in our lives, as definite as the day of our conversion, when we give up all right to ourselves and submit to the absolute Lordship of Jesus Christ. . . . There must be a day when, without reservation, we surrender everything to Him—ourselves, our families, our possessions, our business and our time. All we are and have becomes His, to be held henceforth entirely at His disposal. From that day we are no longer our own masters, but only stewards. Not until the Lordship of Jesus Christ is a settled thing in our hearts can the Holy Spirit really operate effectively in us. He cannot direct our lives until all control of them is committed to Him. If we do not give Him absolute authority in our lives, He can be present, but He cannot be powerful. The power of the Spirit is stayed.

Is today that day for you?

Small Group Study Guide for

BLESSED: EIGHT WAYS CHRISTIANS CHANGE CULTURE

by Ryan Denison

BEFORE YOU BEGIN

Blessed covers the eight Beatitudes contained in Jesus' Sermon on the Mount, but there are ten lessons here: an introductory lesson, eight lessons on each of the Beatitudes, and a concluding lesson.

So as to simplify the schedule for a small group, this guide follows the titling of the book. In other words, if you are leading a small group, you will cover the Introduction in Week 1, followed by Chapter 1 in Week 2, then Chapter 2 in Week 3, and so on.

If you have any questions or suggestions about this guide, contact Denison Forum at comments@denisonforum.org. Be sure that your subject line contains: Blessed small group study guide.

We pray that these words help you and your group go deeper into Jesus' Beatitudes so that your influence for the kingdom may grow wider.

—Denison Forum

STUDY GUIDE SCHEDULE

INTRODUCTION

That our culture is far from perfect should not come as a shock to anyone. For all the benefits that come from being part of this society—and there are many—there is also ample room for improvement.

Unfortunately, our history shows that for every two steps forward, we tend to take at least one step back.

- **Prayerfully think of a few examples to illustrate this point. Racial prejudice, abortion, and poverty are discussed as examples in the book.**

- **Alternatively, you can lead your group in a brief discussion of the topic, but try not to spend more than a few minutes here as it's a subject that can easily overtake the conversation and take the focus down a divisive path that's better avoided.**

- **The purpose is to come away with an understanding of how our culture is both in need of improvement and incapable of getting all the way there on its own.**

In his Sermon on the Mount, Jesus declared to his followers: "You are the salt of the earth . . . You are the light of the world" (Matthew 5:13, 14).

As we'll examine in greater detail soon, *you* is plural, including all Christians. *Are* is in the present tense, describing a fact rather than a prediction or supposition. And *the* makes clear that we are the world's *only* salt and light.

Salt purifies; light dispels darkness. From our Lord's statement, we can know that if our culture is decaying and darkening, the answer is for God's people to become the change agents he intends us to be.

In short, what our culture needs most is a movement of culture-changing Christians.

But what does a culture-changing Christian look like?

What characteristics define someone God is using to impact the culture for Jesus?

Before our Lord defined our calling as salt and light, he first gave us eight statements that answer our question. The Beatitudes tell us precisely how Christians who are changing the culture live—the values and commitments that motivate and inspire them.

As we explore these timeless principles together, our purpose is simple: to align our lives with these eight principles so fully that they define our character and empower our influence.

When we do, we will be the salt and light our Lord desires and our culture desperately needs.

The sermon that changed the world

Read aloud Matthew 5:1–16.

The Beatitudes mark the first real teachings of Jesus in Matthew. Prior to this point, the Gospel records that Jesus had begun to preach a message of repentance and called the disciples to follow him, but Matthew had yet to write down any of his lessons.

As such, in many ways the Beatitudes function as the introduction to Christ's teaching ministry. Along with the rest of the Sermon on the Mount, they create the lens through which we are to view the rest of Jesus' message.

- **Ask your group to discuss how the context of the Beatitudes influences the way we should study these verses.**

- Some points to potentially highlight are:

    1. The Beatitudes and the larger Sermon on the Mount are in many ways a crash course on how to live out the Christian life.

    2. Verses 1 and 2 of Matthew 5 make clear that, while a larger crowd was listening, Jesus was speaking specifically to his disciples with the Sermon. Consequently, the Sermon was intended for people who had already committed to following him. That commitment is a crucial first step in living out these teachings.

In the Sermon on the Mount, Jesus essentially gives his systematic ethic for being his disciples, and this message represents the core of what he taught across three years of public ministry. As such, it must have come as quite a shock when Jesus began his sermon by stating, "Blessed are the poor in spirit, for theirs is the kingdom of heaven."

When he continued with a series of seven additional blessings, all of which were countercultural to the society of his day (and ours), it would have been impossible to avoid the response of those who first heard him: "The crowds were astonished at his teaching, for he was teaching them as one who had authority and not as their scribes" (Matthew 7: 28–29).

You see, contrary to the way in which the Law was presented by most religious leaders of his time, Jesus began his moral instruction by focusing on *character* rather than commands. And until we understand why, we'll never fully grasp the gravity of all the instruction that comes after.

Even if we somehow managed to keep every command found in this sermon but did not exhibit the characteristics described in its first twelve verses, we would never fully experience the blessing of God in our lives.

Nor would we become the salt and light our culture needs.

"Blessed are the . . . ."

Let's now take a closer look at the three points we mentioned briefly in the first section.

First, what Jesus offers us in the Beatitudes is a guide to the kinds of blessings only God can provide.

It's a blessedness that transcends our circumstances; a joy and peace that the world can neither give nor take. We'll learn more about those blessings as we look at each verse in greater detail across subsequent weeks, but, from the start, we must acknowledge that what the Lord offers is something only he can provide.

Secondly, Jesus says, "Blessed *are*."

Not "blessed were," when times were better, or "blessed will be," when your current troubles pass, but "blessed are" because the blessings God uniquely offers are available to you each and every moment of your life. Those who live with the character described in these verses will know and abide in a kind of blessing that too often we mistakenly believe is reserved for heaven (or at least our more peaceful times on earth).

Lastly, he says, "Blessed are *the* . . . ."

In seven of the eight Beatitudes, Jesus begins by using some form of that definitive article to describe those who are blessed. The only exception is when he personalizes those who are persecuted in the final Beatitude.

By starting with some variation of "blessed are the/those," Jesus demonstrates that these characteristics form the only path to the blessing God wants us to have. There is no other way because there could not be another way. The remnants of our fallen nature simply make it too difficult to live every day with the kind of character Jesus describes in these verses.

And, while it will be tempting across our study to focus on those characteristics that come most naturally to us, Jesus did not intend to give us that option.

- **Discuss with your group why that's the case. Why can't we just spend our time and energy trying to maximize our strengths?**

- **What are some practical consequences that such an approach might have when it comes to living out the character of Christ at work, school, home, church, etc.?**

Each of the Beatitudes describes a component of the Christian life without which our character will fall short of the standard to which Jesus has called us. Moreover, we cannot consistently practice some of these traits to the exclusion of the rest. We'll see more about why that's the case as we look at each Beatitude, but for now it's essential that we acknowledge the necessity of each characteristic Jesus chose to include in this part of the Sermon.

The nature of blessing

While it sounds great to live in such a way that we can know the blessing of God, it's worth noting that the same Teacher who offers it also warned us that "in the world you will have tribulation" (John 16:33). Clearly, he did not promise a life free from struggle. In many ways, a life blessed by God will be a more difficult and, at times, less happy existence than what we might make for ourselves.

Happiness is not what Jesus wants most for us, though. Rather, he promises a life of purpose and fulfillment, a sense of well-being that transcends circumstances and makes a genuine difference in the world.

The Beatitudes are, in a sense, Christ's vision for what our lives could be like if we let him be our king. That is not a life of ease, and it will require a kind of self-sacrifice that doesn't always come naturally to us. It is, however, the only way to know the kind of lasting joy and purpose for which we were created. And it's the only way to be the salt and light that will change our culture for God's glory.

- **Close with a time of prayer that God will use the coming week to help each person better understand the degree to which they share the Lord's goals in this regard and that he would give them a desire to pursue the kind of life that exemplifies the character of Christ.**

CHAPTER 1:
Depend on the Spirit

The power of *ptochos*

- **Begin today's lesson by reading Matthew 5:1–3 and then engaging in a brief discussion about what it means to be poor.**

    1. Is poverty strictly a monetary state?

    2. What are some of the other ways we use the term today?

        a. Morally bankrupt, poor sport, etc.

The Greeks had two different words to express the idea of "poor." The one which our Lord used in the Sermon on the Mount is very telling.

The first option was *penes*, which describes a person who has nothing to spare. This is the family living paycheck to paycheck, surviving—but just barely. That is not the word Jesus used.

The second term is *ptochos*, and it describes a person who has nothing at all. This is the family that is starving to death, with no idea where their next meal is coming from. There's a desperation to their state, coupled with a notable lack of hope unless something or someone intercedes on their behalf.

Ptochos is the term Christ used describing the poor in spirit who are blessed. Can you see why those around him must have found his words so perplexing?

The Jews of his day believed that material prosperity was a direct sign of divine blessing. The Romans believed the same. People in both cultures wanted as much financial means as they could possess, seeking to be as wealthy and healthy as possible. The closer they got to reaching that goal, the more it would seem to them and everyone else that God, or the gods, had blessed them.

None would say that a spiritually starving person is blessed. But that's exactly Jesus' claim.

How is this possible?

Those who recognize their absolute need for God and are not dependent on their own circumstances are the only people positioned to receive blessings from God.

When we note the good in our lives and focus on the role we played in attaining it, a fundamental part of its blessing is the sense of pride and accomplishment we feel as a result. However, such an approach focuses on us more than our Lord. Self-sufficiency inevitably makes it harder to make him the king of our lives. (We'll discuss the importance of this step in a moment).

By contrast, those who are poor in spirit see every blessing through the lens of God's role in their lives. Every bit of good leads them back to his throne, and every experience of blessing fills them with gratitude to their Lord.

They do not ignore the role they played in the process of attaining such good, but the primary emotion they feel is gratitude rather than self-satisfaction. This is a fine line, but its importance cannot be overstated.

Jesus definitively states that the poor in spirit will be blessed because only the poor in spirit have fully embraced the reality that a strong relationship with the Lord—one in which he is the king of their lives—is the greatest blessing we can ever receive.

How can we make God our king?

Recognizing God as king

- **Read Luke 20:45–21:4 as a group.**

    1. What can Jesus' warnings about the scribes at the end of chapter 20 and his guidance on who gave the most at the start of chapter 21 teach us about what it means to be poor in spirit?

    2. How did the actions of each group mentioned (scribes, the rich, and the poor widow) demonstrate the manner in which they related to God as their king?

The passage in Luke's gospel offers a good example of the difference between being truly poor in spirit as opposed to mistakenly thinking yourself to be rich in spirit. It's vital to note, however, that the key difference does not reside in the economic state of each figure. The example of early Christians like Barnabas, who was wealthy enough to sell some of his land and donate the proceeds to help his fellow Christians, demonstrates that one can be financially rich while still being poor in spirit (Acts 4:36–37).

What matters is the degree to which our actions illustrate that God is the king of our lives.

The poor in spirit recognize that they need God above everything and everyone else. As a result, seeking his will becomes their highest priority because they see doing so as essential to their spiritual survival.

Unfortunately, such a perspective is as countercultural today as it was two thousand years ago. For many in our society, the Bible is primarily viewed as a diary of religious experiences and God is seen more as a hobby than our king. As a result, we should not be surprised when the kingdom of heaven seems little more than a distant hope for another life.

And while we should expect the lost to embrace such a secular mindset, the greatest tragedy is when this mindset is found within the walls of the church.

Remember: when Jesus first stated that the poor in spirit would be blessed, he spoke most directly to those who claimed to follow him.

The Sermon on the Mount has wisdom for all people, but its target audience is us.

If we want to see the kingdom of heaven made a more

present reality in our culture, then this movement must start with every believer choosing to embrace the kingdom in his or her own life first.

Conclusion

- **Reflect on some of the ways that you first discussed what it means to be poor.**

    1. How does our modern understanding of being poor compare with how the Jews and Romans defined being poor?

    2. How might those similarities make it difficult for us to fully embrace what Jesus is talking about in Matthew 5?

Of all the Beatitudes, this one is perhaps the most foundational. It is also, however, the most surprising and countercultural. As such, being poor in spirit is unlikely to come naturally to us.

So, as you close for today:

- **Discuss practical ways we can better live as "poor in spirit" this week.**

In the *Blessed* book, we recommend four ways:

    1. Submit to the power of the Holy Spirit by making the conscious decision to turn every day over to the Lord.

    2. Measure success spiritually and in accordance with God's priorities.

    3. Measure spirituality by dependence on God.

    4. Measure dependence by obedience.

This list is hardly exhaustive. You and your group would do well to personalize it as much as possible.

- **End with a prayer asking God to help each of you better identify the areas of your life where he is your king and the areas where you are trying to sit on his throne instead.**

- **Close by asking God to help you better embody what it means to be poor in spirit this week.**

CHAPTER 2:
Redeem suffering

- **Begin with a brief discussion on some of the most common reasons people question the existence of a good God.**

  1. While there are many, one of the most common is why a good God would allow so much suffering in the world, especially suffering that was not the result of personal choices.

The purpose of today's lesson is not to explain away those questions about evil and suffering (our book *Making Sense of Suffering* tackles that topic in depth). Rather, the purpose for today is to examine Christ's promise that even in the midst of suffering, we can still experience God's blessing.

- **Read Matthew 5:1–4 as a group.**

Seek to be "blessed"

Last week, we looked at Christ's first promise: "Blessed are the poor in spirit, for theirs is the kingdom of heaven" (Matthew 5:3).

We discussed how that promise is foundational to the rest because the first step in positioning ourselves to receive God's blessing is to recognize our desperate need for him and make him our king in response.

The second Beatitude begins in the same way: "Blessed."

The Greek word used here, *makarios*, means "a sense of well-being that transcends circumstances."

- **Discuss how *makarios* differs from the kind of happiness people often seek in their day-to-day lives.**

    1. Why do you think many people are more prone to pursue happiness than blessing?

Our culture offers happiness based on our happenings, but Jesus offers blessedness based on his grace.

How do we experience it?

We must admit how much we need God and then surrender every facet of our lives to his Lordship.

Expect to mourn

Such blessedness, however, does not insulate us from suffering.

Rather, Jesus treats mourning as an inevitability, with the implication being that we will all have reason to mourn at some point in our lives. Understanding and accepting that

114

reality is vital to experiencing God's blessing because it helps us avoid discouragement or feelings of abandonment during hard times.

Moreover, "mourn" translates the Greek word *penthountes*, which describes a kind of grief so deep that it takes possession of the entire person and cannot be hidden. It's the same word used to describe Jacob's grief upon learning of Joseph's supposed death in Genesis 37:34.

- **Discuss the reasons people might mourn to the depth of *penthountes*.** Some examples discussed in the *Blessed* book include:

  1. Personal losses
  2. Failures or missed opportunities
  3. Sin, whether personal or communal

- **Why might we struggle to be comforted in the midst of such mourning?**

Expect to be comforted

Once we understand the depth of mourning to which Christ refers, we can better understand the gravity of the promise that follows. When Jesus says "they shall be comforted," the Greek literally means "they shall be encouraged" or "they shall be invited in."

But while this promise is unconditional, our experience of it is not guaranteed. The key is that the first Beatitude empowers the second.

When we admit our need for God and bring our grief to him, laying it down at his feet rather than clutching to it (as is so often the case), then we position ourselves to receive his comfort.

When circumstances feel overwhelming, it can be tempting to cling to our grief—at least one thing feels within our control. Doing so, however, often means closing ourselves off to the peace and encouragement we so desperately crave.

If instead we can learn to give our grief to God and then leave it in his hands, he *will* comfort us and work through our circumstances to bring us strength and help.

- **What are some examples from Scripture when Jesus comforted and strengthened the hurting?**

  Below are a few examples included in the *Blessed* book:

  1. Psalm 23:4
  2. Isaiah 49:13
  3. Psalm 34:18
  4. Matthew 11:28–29

Look for ways to comfort others

One way God most often comforts us is by using us to comfort others.

Doing so brings purpose to our pain, and we find community with those who can better understand our grief. It's part of his plan for redeeming our hurt to bring some measure of good from our experiences.

As Paul wrote to the church in Corinth, "Blessed be the God and Father of our Lord Jesus Christ, the Father of mercies and God of all comfort, who comforts us in all our affliction, so that we may be able to comfort those who are in any affliction, with the comfort with which we ourselves are comforted by God" (2 Corinthians 1:3–4).

If you've ever dealt with a personal tragedy, you know how much more helpful those who'd been through something similar could be than those who could only imagine your pain. Now we are called to pay it forward, to help others as we were helped, to be, as Henri Nouwen put it, wounded healers.

- **Finish the lesson with a time of prayer. Ask God to:**

  1. Help you identify hurt or suffering you haven't surrendered to him.

  2. Help you leave that pain at his feet.

  3. Identify anyone in your life for whom your experiences might prove helpful and then guide you to know how to reach out to them.

- **Close by thanking God for his presence during difficult times.**

CHAPTER 3:
Submit to the Lord

- **Read Matthew 5:1–5 as a group.**

In recent weeks, we've discussed the countercultural way Jesus describes the kind of life that God can bless.

We've looked at his promise to bless the poor in spirit: those who are so acutely aware of their need for God that they've made him king over every facet of their lives.

We've also examined his promise to bless those who mourn, experiencing his comfort in the midst of our pain and finding purpose through the avenues it opens for being his hands and feet to the hurting around us.

Today we turn to the third Beatitude: "Blessed are the meek, for they shall inherit the earth" (Matthew 5:5).

- **Discuss what it means to be meek.**

  - What images come to mind?

  - How well do those descriptions match up with someone you think would one day inherit the earth?

We'll spend the rest of our time today discussing how the Bible defines meekness and, in so doing, hopefully come to a better understanding of what Jesus described in Matthew 5:5.

Value humility as God does

The Greek word for "meek" is *praus*, which has been understood historically as humility.

Humility, however, is a concept we often struggle to grasp today.

As such, there are four important steps for understanding the whole of what Jesus characterizes as meekness.

1. Understand what humility is not.

Because we live in a culture that often assigns value based on performance and production, our natural bent is toward trying to impress those around us. It's hard to want to impress people and be humble at the same time, though.

As such, we often mistakenly understand humility as requiring a kind of self-deprecation in which we overvalue our faults to the neglect of what we do well.

- **Ask your group to name some of the ways they've seen this kind of false humility manifest in their lives or in the lives of those they know.**

1. Some possibilities are:

   a. The inability to take a compliment

   b. Hesitance to embrace the areas in which we're gifted

   c. Looking down on others when they don't share this attitude of self-deprecation (This is a particularly dangerous kind of false humility as it not only damages our personal walk with God but can also have a negative impact on our witness.)

As we'll discuss toward the end of this lesson, all of us have been created in the image of God and blessed with incredible gifts to use in advancing his kingdom. It would be strange then for Jesus to say that the key to inheriting that kingdom is ignoring or minimizing those attributes.

At the same time, though, Scripture is clear that taking self-serving pride in those gifts is dangerous as well. That's what makes the second step so important.

2. See yourself as God sees you.

Dr. Martyn Lloyd-Jones defines *praus* as "a humble and gentle attitude to others which is determined by a true estimate of ourselves."

Biblical meekness, then, requires that we understand what that "true estimate" looks like. And there's no better source from which we can acquire that truth than God.

So how does God see us?

- **Ask your group to name some of the ways the Bible describes people.**

1. Some important aspects are:

    a. Sinners who fall short of God's glory (Romans 3:23)

    b. People worthy of eternity in hell (Romans 6:23)

    c. Individuals God loves so much that he deemed their salvation worth the cost of his Son (John 3:16)

    d. If you're a Christian, then you are the adopted child of God and co-heir with Christ (Romans 8:16–17)

Seeing ourselves as God sees us allows us to acknowledge our faults and our gifts without defining ourselves by either. That, in turn, frees us to be truly humble.

Biblical meekness, however, is not just about how we see ourselves.

3. See others as God sees them.

Greek scholar Fritz Rienecker defines *praus* as "The humble and gentle attitude which expresses itself in a patient submissiveness to offense, free from malice and desire for revenge."

To be clear, that doesn't mean refusing to hold others accountable for their mistakes or completely ignoring the wrongs committed against us. Meekness is not weakness.

Rather, it means not defining people by their mistakes or offenses against us.

Just as we learned in the previous step to see ourselves as God sees us, defining our identity by our relationship with him, so too we must extend that same grace to others. As Paul instructed the Ephesians, "Be kind to one another, tenderhearted, forgiving one another, as God in Christ forgave you" (Ephesians 4:32).

This kind of forgiveness requires a level of humility that does not come naturally to our fallen natures. It's also not possible if our humility is based on anything other than our standing before the Lord.

After all, if we forgive out of obligation, then some shred of resentment is likely to remain no matter what we say. That resentment will also remain if our understanding of forgiveness is to simply brush off an offense as if nothing happened.

Only true humility—biblical meekness—will enable us to model to others the kind of forgiveness God has shown toward us.

4. See your gifts as God sees them.

The final step in positioning ourselves to experience the blessing Jesus promised to the meek is to see our gifts and abilities as God sees them.

James Montgomery Boice gives, perhaps, my favorite definition of *praus*: "power put under control." He likens it to a powerful stallion submitted to the control of its rider.

The stallion's strength, speed, and abilities are not lessened because it has learned to follow its master's lead. Rather, in many ways they are enhanced because its wild nature is more easily focused toward a particular end.

The same happens when we take the gifts and abilities God has instilled in each of us and present them back to him as a living sacrifice (Romans 12:1).

True meekness means embracing our gifts and talents as a blessing from God, then submitting them to his service.

When we do, genuine humility is no longer an ideal we have to pursue but instead a natural byproduct of our walk with God.

Conclusion

We've examined four different steps to becoming biblically meek.

As we've seen, each comprises a different, yet equally vital, aspect of genuine humility.

- **In closing, discuss which of the four steps seems most difficult to practice on a daily basis and why.**

  1. Then discuss some practical steps you can take this week to help overcome those difficulties.

  2. When you're done, close in prayer, asking God to help you live in such a way that you can experience the blessing of biblical meekness.

CHAPTER 4:
Value Integrity

- **Read Matthew 5:1–6 as a group.**

Today's lesson will focus on Christ's fourth Beatitude: "Blessed are those who hunger and thirst for righteousness, for they shall be satisfied" (Matthew 5:6).

As we'll soon see, though, satisfaction is not always an easy concept for us to understand. And when we seek satisfaction from the wrong places, it can make prioritizing righteousness all but impossible.

What do you want?

When Jesus spoke of hunger and thirst, the concept was far more real to his audience than it is for many of us today.

Relatively few people had the security of starting the day knowing they would have enough to eat for dinner that night. Even when they did, it was rarely to the point of being full.

When Jesus fed the five thousand, for example, the fact that the crowds were "satisfied" was as amazing to some as the way in which Jesus had provided the food (Matthew 14:13–21).

Our society has largely reached the point where, even when food is scarce, it's rarely to the point of starvation (though, tragically, that is not always the case).

However, all of us hunger and thirst for something to a comparable degree.

- **Ask your group to name what people hunger and thirst for today. What, if anything, do they have in common?**

  1. Some examples given in the *Blessed* book are:

     a. Raising successful children

     b. Retiring comfortably

     c. Getting into the right school

     d. Having the right friends

     e. Being "happy"

Ultimately, we pursue these things because we think that achieving them will bring us some level of satisfaction that makes them worth the cost.

However, Jesus argues that the kind of satisfaction we really need can only come from the Lord, and he's quite clear on how to get it.

What should you want?

The Greek word translated here as "righteousness" is *dikaiosynen*. It conveys the basic ideas of justice and integrity.

However, before we seek righteousness in the world around us, we have to seek it in our personal lives.

- **Ask the group to give some examples, either from the Bible or current events, of people who were righteous in action but not in character. (If you discuss current events, prevent the conversation from devolving into gossip or politics.)**

    1. Potential examples are:

        a. The religious leaders in Jesus' day

        b. When Israel offered sacrifices to God without a penitent heart

        c. Countless pastors and modern-day leaders who lost their ministry due to moral failings

While we must start with the internal part of righteousness, Scripture is also clear that personal righteousness is incomplete unless it manifests in the pursuit of justice and caring for others.

Micah 6:8 epitomizes this balance well: "He has told you, O man, what is good; and what does the Lord require of you but to do justice, and to love kindness, and to walk humbly with your God?"

If we want to walk in close communion with God, then we have to care about the same things he does.

That means hungering and thirsting for righteousness in our personal lives and in the world around us. Trying to do one without the other, though, dooms our efforts to failure.

- **Ask: Why do we need to be righteous in our personal lives if we want to effectively advance righteousness in the world around us?**

With that discussion in mind, let's turn to the final part of our lesson.

How do we achieve righteousness?

The first step is to *decide that we want to be righteous.*

That may seem obvious, but to truly hunger and thirst for righteousness as if we would die without it takes a level of daily devotion that does not come naturally to most of us.

There will be days when we simply lack the drive to pursue justice and integrity to that degree. Unfortunately, those are often the times when we are most likely to make a choice that jeopardizes the work we've done and the equity we've built up in better days.

That's why the second step is also crucial: *admit that you are not righteous without God.*

It's important to note that Jesus didn't say "blessed are those who are righteous," but rather "blessed are those who hunger and thirst for righteousness."

This side of heaven, none of us will be truly righteous.

But the inevitability of our failures is no reason to accept them. Rather, it's a reminder that our righteousness is ultimately dependent upon the power of the Holy Spirit in our lives. And, as Paul told the Galatians, if we want to experience the fruit of the Spirit in our lives, then we have to "keep in step with the Spirit" (Galatians 5:16–25).

When we do, the third step takes place: *we find satisfaction in the Lord.*

Jesus was clear that when we hunger and thirst for righteousness, we will be filled. Note, however, that his promise was in the passive tense. God's blessing fills us; we don't fill ourselves. That's why we will never find true and lasting satisfaction apart from the Lord. It's simply not possible without him.

Yes, we can find fleeting moments of happiness and even sate our hunger for purpose and fulfillment for a time through any number of avenues. But it won't last. Jesus is still our only source for living water (John 4).

Conclusion

Today we've looked at what it means to truly hunger and thirst for righteousness, as well as why that is the only avenue to true satisfaction.

- **In closing, discuss some practical ways you can better position yourselves to experience the blessing of righteousness this week.**

- **When you're done, close in prayer, asking God to help you prioritize righteousness in your personal life and in your interactions with others this week.**

CHAPTER 5:
Choose to Pardon

- **Begin today's lesson with a brief discussion about how you define mercy.**

    1. Perhaps contrast it with grace: Grace is getting what you don't deserve; mercy is not getting what you do deserve.

In our passage for today, we're going to look at Christ's promise that those who are merciful will be blessed by receiving mercy in turn.

As we'll see, though, that mercy may not always look like what we'd expect.

What is mercy?

- **Ask someone to read Matthew 5:1–7 to the group.**

Often, the best way to define mercy is to start by defining what it's not.

Ethicist Lewis Smedes gives four examples of common misconceptions when it comes to showing mercy (or, as it's more commonly understood, forgiveness):

1. Forgiving is not forgetting.

While God promises that when we confess, he "remembers your sins no more" (Isaiah 43:25), you and I cannot do that in most cases. Our minds are not hard drives we can just wipe when they contain something we'd rather not remember. As such, a key component of being merciful is figuring out how not to hold a grudge over a wrong we cannot forget.

2. Forgiving is not excusing the behavior that hurt you.

A common response when someone apologizes is "That's all right" when it really wasn't. While it may seem simplistic, learning to say "I forgive you" instead really can go a long way toward helping both parties move past the incident. This is especially important when it comes to conversations with children about mercy.

3. Forgiving is not pretending you're not hurt.

Smedes' third point echoes his second. Ignoring the pain doesn't make it go away. Rather, it drives the hurt down deeper, where the roots can grow and stretch out to other corners of our lives in ways that are both difficult to trace and untangle.

4. *Forgiving is not tolerating.*

While toleration may be among the chief ideals of our culture today, it's a cheap replacement for genuine forgiveness. If you doubt that's the case, tell the people you care about "I tolerate you" and see their reaction. As Christians, we can and should set a much higher standard for our treatment of others.

Rather, to forgive is to pardon.

It's to refuse to punish, even though you have every right to do so. It's seeking to reestablish a relationship with them that takes into account what was done (to avoid setting ourselves up for it to happen again), but without allowing that wrong to remain an impediment to real community.

In short, mercy means choosing not to define someone by their worst mistakes, just as God has chosen not to use that standard against us.

Taking that step is seldom easy, though.

So why should we make the effort, especially if we think the other person isn't really sorry for their part in our pain?

Why should you be merciful?

- **Discuss why we should be merciful. Where possible, reference examples or passages from Scripture to show why forgiveness is necessary.**

  1. Some examples from the *Blessed* book are:

     a. To stop your personal cycle of pain: Every time you hold onto a grudge, you also hold onto the pain of that initial hurt. The only way to make the cycle of pain stop is to forgive.

b. Pardon to receive mercy: It's not that God isn't willing to forgive us if we don't forgive others, but rather that we are not positioned to receive his mercy without being merciful to others.

c. Pardon to break the circle of revenge: If I hurt you in response to you hurting me, it is likely to create a cycle that can only be broken when one person chooses to forgive rather than retaliate.

d. To show others the love of Christ: In John 13:35, Jesus says, "By this everyone will know you are my disciples, if you love one another." When we respond to a hurt with the love and forgiveness God has shown us, we point people to him.

Understanding that forgiveness is necessary does not make it easy to give, though.

So let's finish our lesson with four practical steps we can take to be more merciful.

How can you be merciful?

1. Admit the reality of your hurt.

For many of us, we don't want to admit to having been hurt. Why? Because pain can make us feel weak or "less than," as if we're ashamed for allowing ourselves to have been hurt in the first place.

I believe that's why many people pretend that a hurtful issue is "no big deal." They don't want to admit to having been hurt by something that others might see as inconsequential. Neither do they want to admit the pain and live it all over again.

So the one in pain tries to quickly move past the issue—but the hurt still remains.

It can be tempting to try to act as though we're not bothered by pain or that we've moved past it before we really have. As we discussed before, though, ignoring the pain doesn't make it go away. Admitting it to ourselves and, ultimately, to God is a necessary first step to both extending and receiving his mercy.

2. Ask God to help you pardon the one who hurt you.

The Beatitudes are addressed to believers because God knows that we could never live up to these standards without him. While he doesn't expect us to, he's also not going to help if we won't ask.

That's also why the Beatitudes are sequential. If we admit our need of God and mourn for our own sins, living under the control of the Spirit and seeking to be righteous in every relationship, then we can be empowered to extend to others the mercy Christ has extended to us.

So, turn to the Holy Spirit.

Ask him for the power and pardon of God.

Ask him for the ability to see this person as he does and to see yourself as he does—both of you redeemed sinners.

Ask him to help you extend to your enemy the mercy God has given to you.

And, finally, act as though he has, reminding yourself that you have forgiven the other person every time Satan tries to bring the hurt back up.

3. Initiate restoration.

Jesus taught us to go directly to the person who sins against us (Matthew 18:15). Once you have decided to forgive the other person, reach out to them and let them in on your process. If I hurt you, I want to know it. I want you to talk to me, not about me. And I to you.

However, you must forgive them before taking this step or else your mercy will invariably be conditioned by their response. Remember, forgiveness is me giving up the right to hurt you for hurting me. Mercy is not earned by the other person's repentance.

Hopefully, that conversation goes well and the other person is truly penitent for the wrong they've done. But that will never be guaranteed. If our forgiveness is contingent upon their response, then we're unlikely to ever truly forgive.

4. Be realistic.

Forgiveness is hard, and we delude ourselves if we think otherwise. Time and practice can make it easier, but the greatest help comes from remembering how often we've been forgiven, both by other people and by our heavenly Father.

And if mercy is something you've struggled to accept or give in the past, then being realistic about your progress will be even more important.

Conclusion

- **Close your time by discussing which of the four steps outlined above has historically proven the most difficult to practice consistently. Why do you think that's the case?**

- **Finish by leading everyone in a time of prayer and silent reflection when they ask God:**

  1. To bring to mind anyone to whom they need to show mercy

  2. To bring to mind anyone from whom they need ask for forgiveness

  3. To help them walk through these four steps faithfully as they seek to experience mercy this week

CHAPTER 6:
Love God and People

- **Begin your discussion by recapping key points from the previous weeks.**

- Some points to potentially emphasize are:

  1. With the Beatitudes, Jesus provided believers with a systematic ethic for how to be his disciples that focused on building Christlike character rather than following a particular set of commands.

  2. The blessings often build on one another, with the first Beatitude's emphasis on making God our king foundational to the rest.

  3. The characteristics Jesus describes throughout these verses are often countercultural and counter to our inherent sin nature. As such, they're not qualities that are likely to develop in us without a conscious and intentional effort on

our part to help them grow in conjunction with the Holy Spirit's presence in our lives.

4. As we'll see in today's lesson, understanding the steps we've taken to reach this point is important for fully grasping what it means to be pure in heart.

Choose to have a life purpose

- **Read Matthew 5:1–8 to the group.**

Greek scholar Fritz Rienecker defines "heart" as "the center of the inner life of the person where all the spiritual forces and functions have their origin." In addition, "pure" refers to a consistent, focused integrity.

So, to be "pure in heart" essentially means to live in such a way that every facet of your life is guided by a consistent and Christ-centered integrity. What that looks like practically is that our outward actions mirror our inward state in a way that demonstrates God's presence in our lives.

Jesus spoke to this principle again when warning against the hypocrisy of the religious leaders.

- **Read Matthew 23:25–28.**

- **What is it about the scribes and Pharisees that Jesus warns against in these verses? How might that warning pertain to our discussion of what it means to have a pure heart?**

On any given day, most of us only have the margin to clean the inside or the outside of Christ's proverbial cup and plate. Either we focus on appearing clean and well put together for those looking on, or we spend our time trying to make sure our hearts are right with the Lord.

Which purpose we choose to make our primary emphasis will determine whether we stand before God as a whitewashed tomb or a holy vessel that reflects his influence on our lives. And Jesus is clear that only one of those options will result in the blessing of God's abiding presence.

So, what practical steps can we take to live every day pure in heart?

Choose the right life purpose

In the chapter just before Christ's condemnation of the religious leaders that we examined earlier, the Pharisees tried to test Jesus by asking him to narrow down all 613 commandments they held dear to the most important.

- **Ask someone in the group to read that encounter from Matthew 22:34–40.**

- **What from Christ's response can give us some practical guidelines for living with the kind of pure heart we've discussed today?**

   1. The *Blessed* book goes into more detail on what it means to love God with all our heart, soul, and mind and to love our neighbor as ourselves, but it essentially comes down to pursuing God as our primary focus—loving him with every facet of our lives—and then embodying his presence and love to the world around us.

Choosing the pursuit of God as our primary purpose in life enables us to "see God" in a way nothing else will.

The Greek word for "see" is *horao*, and it refers to far more than simple sight. Rather, it implies an experience or sense of perception. As such, when Jesus promised that the pure in heart would see God, he promised that they would know the indwelling presence of the Lord in an intimate and personal way.

And this experience does not have to wait until we get to heaven. For those who are pure in heart, the eternal presence of our holy and infinite God can be part of our lives every minute of every day.

In fact, it should be.

Conclusion

As we've discussed in previous weeks, these Beatitudes were intended to be a guidebook for believers to experience God's daily blessing, but the only way we could possibly live them out consistently is by depending on the Lord to help us do so.

In that sense, Christ can promise that only the pure in heart will see God because the process of becoming and remaining pure in heart places us in God's presence.

Conversely, if our focus is on looking like a good Christian rather than taking the necessary steps to become one, we will not see God because we've fixed our eyes on ourselves instead.

- **Close with a time of prayer. Have everyone take a few minutes and ask God:**

  1. To help them understand in what ways they might be more focused on cleaning the outside than the inside of their spiritual cups

2. To help them love God with their heart, soul, and mind and love their neighbors as themselves

3. To have a renewed longing to experience God in a personal way and to have the discipline and humility necessary to make that experience a daily priority

CHAPTER 7:
Seek Peace

It's been estimated that, in the last 3,400 years, humans have been entirely at peace for 268 of them, constituting 8 percent of human history.

In truth, that likely just means there have been 268 years where our records aren't all that good.

It's no secret that our world lacks peace. In our lesson for today, we'll learn about how God has called us to play a key role in helping people find peace.

However, we can't help other people find peace until we've experienced it in our own lives first.

Fortunately, Scripture has a good bit to say on both topics.

Make peace with God

- **Read Matthew 5:1–9 as a group.**

- **Discuss how you define peace.**

- **How do people look for peace in the world today?**

Scripture makes clear that true peace—the kind that is more than a fleeting absence of conflict—is a gift from God.

Jesus told his disciples, "I have said these things to you that in me you may have peace. In the world you will have tribulation. But take heart; I have overcome the world" (John 16:33).

Paul says that peace is one of the fruits of the Spirit (Galatians 5:22) and, as such, is the result of the Spirit's work in our lives rather than a product of human effort.

If we want to experience God's peace, though, we have to position ourselves to receive it. And the first step in that process is admitting we need his help.

For many Christians, this is a step that's easily taken for granted. After all, a relationship with Christ has to start with admitting our need for him. Once we've done that, though, it can be easy to go through our day-to-day existence relying more on ourselves than on the Lord.

That's not to say he wants us to just sit back and watch him work, but we'll never grow so strong in our faith that we move beyond our need for his power and presence. And trying to do God's work without God's power can be an immense source of stress and frustration, two of the most common impediments to real peace.

It's not enough, though, to simply admit that we need the Lord's help. We must then do what's necessary to receive it, which starts by spending time with him.

What that time looks like is between you and the Lord, and it may change from month to month or even day to day. Giving God the freedom to direct that time, though, will help to reinforce your reliance on him while also giving him the room to guide you to whatever avenues he knows will best bring his peace into your life.

It might be that your challenges for today require extra time spent in prayer and reflection. Tomorrow might bring trials for which you could use a few extra minutes digging into Scripture.

Only God can know for sure, though, and if we want to know his peace in the midst of trying times, relying on his guidance is essential.

Christ's promise in this Beatitude, however, was not "Blessed are those who are at peace" but rather "Blessed are the peacemakers."

So, once we've experienced the peace of God, how do we go about sharing that with others?

Make peace with others

One of the best examples of a peacemaker in Scripture is Jonathan.

- **Ask someone in the group to read 1 Samuel 19:1–7.**

- **What are some aspects of what Jonathan did in this passage that we can apply to our own lives to be better peacemakers?**

147

1. Possible examples are:

    a. Jonathan was the calmest voice in the conversation. David was scared because Saul was trying to kill him. Saul was enraged because he felt threatened by David. But Jonathan was able to speak calmly and rationally to both men.

    b. Jonathan made peace his top priority. One of the reasons Saul felt threatened by David is that he understood how the latter's popularity was a threat to not only his throne but his son's as well. In making peace between Saul and David, Jonathan had to set aside what could have been the clearest path to rule.

    c. Jonathan saw the situation through to the point of reconciliation. It wasn't enough for Jonathan to simply assuage his father's anger or his friend's fear. Rather, he took the added step of bringing the two of them back together and trying to restore their relationship.

One final reason why Jonathan's example is helpful is that, even though he brought about peace in this instance, it wouldn't last. Saul would eventually go back to trying to kill David. By that point, there was nothing Jonathan could do to bring them back together.

In the same way, there will be times when we try to make peace and it simply doesn't work. As we discussed with the Beatitude about mercy, though, we are not ultimately responsible for others' choices. But even when peace seems like a longshot, Scripture requires us to try.

And Christ promises that when we do, we will be called the children of God.

Notice, however, that Jesus does not say we will *become* the children of God. That is not a title we can earn through works but rather one that God bestows on us when we accept Christ as our Lord and Savior. Instead, when we embody the peace of God and try to share it with others, we demonstrate the kind of love and concern that identifies us as his disciples (John 13:35).

Conclusion

Peace is a rare and elusive quality in our culture today. Part of the reason, as we discussed at the start of the lesson, is that people are often more interested in avoiding conflict than experiencing true peace.

As Christians, we have the opportunity to help them want something better, but it will only happen if they see it in us first.

- **As you close the lesson, discuss practical ways you can be peacemakers this week. What are some potential obstacles to look out for in that pursuit?**

- **Finish by closing in prayer, asking the Lord to help you take advantage of those opportunities and avoid those dangers.**

CHAPTER 8:
Serve Christ with Courage

According to Gary Bauer, commissioner of the US Commission of International Religious Freedom (USCIRF), "Christians are the most persecuted religious group in the world, and it's accelerating."

While 30 percent of the world's population identifies as Christian, 80 percent of all acts of religious discrimination around the world are directed at Christians.

One scholar estimates that 90 percent of all people killed on the basis of their religious beliefs are Christians.

The USCIRF has identified sixteen countries where "heinous and systematic" offenses, including torture, imprisonment, and murder, occur against religious communities. The only religion under attack in all sixteen countries is Christianity.

And while not every form of persecution Christians face is likely to rise to the level of "heinous and systematic" offenses, Jesus warned us not to be surprised when we face opposition for our faith.

But if such opposition is inevitable, our focus needs to be less on lamenting its existence and more on figuring out how to endure it well.

Today's lesson will focus on learning how to do just that.

Expect persecution

- **Ask someone in the group to read Matthew 5:1–12.**

- **Discuss what persecution most often looks like in your context.**

When you compare the persecution you've faced to the trials endured by Christians in China, North Korea, or areas of the Middle East, does part of you feel guilty even calling it persecution? If so, that's an understandable response.

It's worth noting, however, that when we look back at the early Christians, their persecution often looked a lot more like ours than we might think.

While the horrific examples—being fed to the lions, burned at the stake, torn limb-from-limb, etc.—get the most attention, the truth is that times of intense persecution in the early church were fairly rare. With the exception of a few particularly bad years, such instances were mostly regional and limited to when the Romans needed a scapegoat for a lost battle or natural disaster.

Consider that Peter preached for thirty years before he was killed; Paul preached and traveled for fifteen to twenty years before his martyrdom. Recall too that the book of Acts encompasses twenty to thirty years of early church history. Episodes of life-threatening persecution occurred—but not consistently. And Acts 15 recounts how the early church held a large gathering of the early Christian leaders, and none of them seemed concerned with being raided or sent to jail.

While the threat of death was always present, it really wasn't something that most early believers had to worry about. Rather, most of the time the persecution they endured was more in the form of slander, gossip, and ridicule. Enemies of Christ said "all kinds of evil" against them because it was easier to mischaracterize their beliefs than to understand their faith.

Early Christians were called cannibals, for example, because they shared a meal that symbolized the body and blood of Christ. They were accused of sexual perversion because they called that meal the "love feast" while inviting prostitutes and referring to one another as brothers and sisters in the Lord. Because they refused to bow before a bust of the emperor and say "Caesar is Lord," they were accused of atheism and treason.

Early Christians endured scorn from those around them because it was easier for non-Christians to believe the worst stereotypes and misconceptions than risk having to grapple with the truth of our faith. This kind of persecution was, in large part, what Jesus had in mind when he said, "Blessed are those who are persecuted because of righteousness."

While a day may very well come when we're asked to endure far more for our faith than slander and ridicule, learning how to remain righteous in the face of such mistreatment is just as important for us today as it was for those first generations of believers.

Evaluate your courage

The first step in enduring such trials is to realize that not all persecution is because of righteousness.

Some of the stereotypes against Christians exist because they're true. We can be overly judgmental. We can be closed minded. And we can be hypocritical.

We are human, after all, and all humans are prone to those sins.

Christians get into trouble when we blind ourselves to sin by believing the pushback we receive is a sign that we're walking with God.

A better path when we face persecution is to first take a step back and ask God to help us honestly evaluate why we are being harassed.

To that end, we can find some helpful guidance in the book of Daniel.

- **Read Daniel 6:1–5 in your group.**

- **What stands out most about Daniel in this passage?**

- **What can we take from this example to help us better evaluate when we suffer for the sake of righteousness and when we suffer for a different reason?**

Daniel lived a life of such integrity that those who wished him harm came to the conclusion that the only way they could trap him was "in connection with the law of his God."

If you wonder whether or not the discrimination, slander, gossip, or other trials you face are the result of your commitment to righteousness, checking those reasons against the teachings of Scripture is a very good place to start.

And understand that there are times where we can be unrighteous in our pursuit of righteousness.

As a result, it's essential for us to remember that the law of our God, especially as explained by Jesus, was often focused as much on the heart behind our actions as the actions themselves.

It's not OK to be a jerk just because you think you're doing it for Jesus. Any action God calls you to take in the pursuit of righteousness can be done in a righteous and Christ-honoring way.

But when we do, Jesus promises that we will find ourselves in a long line of those who were willing to forgo the praise of people in order to receive the appreciation of God forever.

Conclusion

Enduring the scorn and persecution of others for the sake of Christ takes a level of courage and commitment that cannot be developed in the moment of trial.

Rather, it requires a life of daily dedication to the pursuit of righteousness, like Jesus modeled for us throughout the gospels.

- **As you close the lesson, reserve the last few minutes to discuss practical steps you can take this week to both evaluate the true reasons behind any persecution you're facing now and set in place some practices to help ensure that any mistreatment you face in the future will be for the sake of righteousness.**

- End your time by praying that God will help you prepare now for when times of persecution come and to help you live every day with Daniel's commitment to the Lord so that others cannot find any grounds for complaint against you except in connection with the teachings of God.

CHAPTER 9:
Changed People
Change the World

Across the last nine weeks, we've examined each of the Beatitudes in detail, noting what qualities and characteristics best equip us to live a life God can bless. It's important to remember, though, that when Jesus taught the Beatitudes to his followers, they were an introduction to a much larger conversation.

As we discussed at the start of our study, the Beatitudes are meant to help us understand how to live, not only so that we can experience God's blessings but also so that we can then become a blessing to the world around us.

To that end, Jesus followed his final statement of blessing with one of calling.

- **Read Matthew 5:1–16 as a group.**

- **It might be helpful to assign each verse or set of verses to a different person as follows:** Matthew 5:1–3, 5:4, 5:5, 5:6, 5:7, 5:8, 5:9, 5:10–12, 5:13–16.

A call to be present

As countercultural principles that are difficult for us to live out on any given day, the Beatitudes would seem much easier to keep if we separated ourselves from the world.

Christians have tried that from time to time across the years. Monasteries, for example, started in large part as a way for a select group of Christians to live out their faith in theoretical safety from the temptations and harsher elements of life that made it difficult for the masses to follow Christ devoutly. Part of their job was to preserve the faith for everyone else.

Of course, monks were still people, so simply secluding themselves from society did not inoculate them against sin. In the end, monasticism's most enduring legacy often had less to do with preserving the faith than with taking the most devoted followers of Christ and removing them from the general public. One might say they hid their light under a bowl and the world around them often suffered as a result.

There are some today who look at the state of the culture around us and argue that Christians should do something similar: we should mostly withdraw from the larger society to protect our faith until a time when the world is more receptive to it. The temptation to do so is understandable.

Jesus, however, was clear that we have been called to a different kind of life—one lived in the world but not of the world, as Billy Graham put it.

But if we are to do so effectively, it will require a daily commitment to a lifestyle defined by heaven's standards rather than our own. In short, it requires a Beatitudes approach to life.

The irony is that it's only by living in a way that runs counter to our fallen natures that we can become what Jesus says we already are.

Remember, he told his followers: you *are* the salt of the earth and you *are* the light of the world. These are not descriptions of what they might one day become but rather inherent characteristics of their identity as his disciples.

As countercultural as a Beatitudes way of life may seem, it is exactly who God created us to be and exactly what our culture desperately needs us to be.

- **Allocate the remainder of the lesson to unpacking what God has taught you and the members of the group from the Beatitudes over the last nine weeks.**

- It may be helpful to go over each Beatitude in turn, time permitting, or leave it open to general conversation. Some summary notes on each Beatitude from the *Blessed* book are:

  1. "Blessed are the poor in spirit, for theirs is the kingdom of heaven" (v. 3): We begin every day by submitting to the Holy Spirit, seeking his empowering and leading through our life and service.

  2. "Blessed are those who mourn, for they shall be comforted" (v. 4): We stand with those who suffer, showing God's love in our compassion.

  3. "Blessed are the meek, for they shall inherit the earth" (v. 5): We submit daily to God's control, trusting him to use our gifts and opportunities to advance his kingdom.

4. "Blessed are those who hunger and thirst for righteousness, for they shall be satisfied" (v. 6): We seek to be people of personal integrity so the Spirit can use us and others will see Christ in us.

5. "Blessed are the merciful, for they shall receive mercy" (v. 7): As an example of God's grace, we choose to pardon those who have hurt us.

6. "Blessed are the pure in heart, for they shall see God" (v. 8): We live for the singular purpose of loving God and others with passion and joy.

7. "Blessed are the peacemakers, for they shall be called sons of God" (v. 9): We choose to be at peace with God, others, and ourselves so as to offer God's peace to our fallen world.

8. "Blessed are those who are persecuted for righteousness' sake, for theirs is the kingdom of heaven" (v. 10): We face the opposition of our culture with courage and joy.

As we conclude our study, remember that our ultimate purpose is not to be good people or live a life God can bless but rather to point people to God (v. 16).

As long as that remains our focus, however, the rest will fall into place much more naturally.

- **Conclude the lesson by praying that God will help you use what you've learned across the course of this study to live a life that points people back to him. Highlight a few of the main points people brought up in the discussion time above.**

About the Authors

DR. JIM DENISON speaks and writes on cultural and contemporary issues facing our world today. He is a trusted author and subject matter expert in areas where faith and current events intersect. His free *Daily Article* is distributed by email to hundreds of thousands around the world and provides leading insight for discerning today's news from a biblical perspective.

Whether it's through *The Daily Article*, speaking engagements, website articles, or social media, Denison Forum is a go-to resource to help readers discern the news differently.

Dr. Denison is the author of multiple books and has taught philosophy of religion and apologetics for over thirty years with four seminaries and in multiple countries. Currently, he serves as Resident Scholar for Ethics with Baylor Scott & White Health, where he addresses issues such as genetic medicine and reproductive science. He is a Senior Fellow with the 21st Century Wilberforce Initiative, where he addresses issues related to politics and religious liberty. He also serves as Senior Fellow for Global Studies at Dallas Baptist University's Institute for Global Engagement. In addition, he chairs the DBU Advisory Board, teaches doctoral seminars, and frequently speaks on campus.

Prior to founding the Denison Forum in 2009, Dr. Denison served as pastor of churches in Dallas, Atlanta and Midland. He earned a Doctor of Philosophy and Master of Divinity from Southwestern Baptist Theological Seminary, and received a Doctor of Divinity from Dallas Baptist University.

Jim and his wife Janet live in Dallas, Texas, and have two sons and four grandchildren.

RYAN DENISON is the Senior Fellow for Theology at Denison Forum. He consults on *The Daily Article* and provides writing and research for many of the ministry's productions.

He is in the final stages of earning his PhD in church history at BH Carroll Theological Institute after having earned his MDiv at Truett Seminary. Ryan has also taught at BH Carroll and Dallas Baptist University.

He and his wife, Candice, live in East Texas and have two children.

About Denison Ministries

DENISON MINISTRIES exists to create culture-changing Christians who are committed to advancing the kingdom through that sphere of influence.

We aspire to influence 3 million Christians every day:

- to speak into real life through daily cultural commentary at DenisonForum.org

- to experience God through a daily devotional resource at First15.org

- and to bring Jesus into parenting moments at ChristianParenting.org

To contact Denison Ministries, email us at comments@ denisonforum.org.

Notes

INTRODUCTION

1   **a majority of Americans believe race relations in the United States are bad:** Juliana Menasce Horowitz, Anna Brown, and Kiana Cox, "How Americans see the state of race relations," *Pew Research Center*, last modified April 9, 2019, https://www.pewsocialtrends.org/2019/04/09/how-americans-see-the-state-of-race-relations/.

2   **percentage of Americans living in poverty:** "Poverty rate in the United States from 1990 to 2017," *statista,* last modified April 29, 2019, https://www.statista.com/statistics/200463/us-poverty-rate-since-1990/.

2   **For black infants:** Katherine Paschall, Tamara Halle, and Jessica Dym Bartlett, "Poverty rate rising among America's youngest children, particularly infants of color," *Child Trends*, last modified September 14, 2018, https://www.childtrends.org/poverty-rate-rising-among-americas-youngest-children-particularly-infants-of-color.

2   **Minorities had higher poverty rates:** Steven Pressman, "The Range of Poverty in America," *U.S. News & World Report*, last modified September 12, 2018, https://www.usnews.com/news/healthiest-communities/articles/2018-09-12/poverty-in-america-new-census-data-paint-an-unpleasant-picture.

2   **abortions in the United States:** Jessica Ravitz, "Abortion rates in US reach a decade low, CDC reports," *CNN*, last modified November 21, 2018, https://www.cnn.com/ 2018/11/21/health/abortion-surveillance-cdc-2015-bn/index.html.

2   **the movement to legitimize:** An example is the profane, graphic article by Sarah Miller, "The Best Abortion Ever," *The Cut*, last modified June 19, 2019, https://www.thecut.com/2019/06/the-best-abortion-ever.html.

5   **given as one sermon or is rather a summary of his teachings:** Valid arguments can be made for both views, but the issue is ultimately irrelevant to the Sermon's meaning and importance.

5   **As St. Augustine notes:** http://www.newadvent.org/ fathers/16011.htm (Augustine, *On the Sermon on the Mount*, Vol. 1. Chapter 1.1).

CHAPTER 1

11   **Our planet is estimated to weigh:** "How much does Earth weigh and how is this measured?" *Cool Cosmos*, http://coolcosmos.ipac.caltech.edu/ask/61-How-much-does-Earth-weigh-and-how-is-this-measured-.

11   **To move it even one millionth of a meter:** "Can you move the Earth with a lever?" *Dedoimedo*, https://www.dedoimedo.com/physics/archimedes-lever.html.

12 **Earth is just one of approximately:** Ethan Siegel, "How Many Planets Are In The Universe?" *ScienceBlogs*, last modified January 5, 2013, https://scienceblogs.com/startswithabang/2013/01/05/how-many-planets-are-in-the-universe, accessed 21 June 2019.

19 **C. S. Lewis:** C. S. Lewis, *The Weight of Glory* (New York: HarperOne, 2001).

CHAPTER 2

22 **see my book, *Wrestling with God*:** James Denison, *Wrestling with God: How Can I Love a God I'm Not Sure I Trust?* (Carol Stream, IL: SaltRiver, 2008).

22 **my website article:** Jim Denison, "Why does a good God allow an evil world? *Denison Forum*, modified July 28, 2011, https://www.denisonforum.org/resource/faith-questions/why-does-a-good-god-allow-an-evil-world/.

27 **Dwight Moody was right:** William R. Moody, *D.L. Moody* (Chicago: Moody Press, 2013).

28 **A. B. Simpson noted:** *Sermon Illustrations*, http://www.sermonillustrations.com/a-z/t/trials.htm

28 **Here's how he later described his condition:** Augustine, *Confessions* (Indianapolis: Hackett Publishing Company, 2006), 8:5.

28 **Gordon MacDonald was a successful pastor:** Richard Exley, "Handling Sexual Temptation," *Christianity Today*, last modified 1994, https://www.

christianitytoday.com/pastors/leadership-books/
dangerstoils/mmpp05-9.html.

29   **In her best-seller,** *The Hiding Place***:** Corrie ten Boom, *The Hiding Place*, 35th Anniversary ed. (Grand Rapids: Chosen Books, 2006), 247.

CHAPTER 3

34   **A. W. Tozer:** A. W. Tozer, *God Tells the Man Who Cares: God Speaks to Those Who Take Time to Listen* (Hannibal, MO: Wingspread, 2006).

34   **St. Augustine:** Quoted in Everett L. Worthington Jr., *Humility: The Quiet Virtue* (West Conshohocken, PA: Templeton Press, 2007), 48

34   **C. S. Lewis:** C. S. Lewis, *Mere Christianity* (Grand Rapids: Zondervan, 2001), 124.

35   **Consider this profound statement:** Paul Tournier, *The Strong and the Weak* (Eugene, OR: Wipf & Stock, 2013), 20.

37   **Dr. Martyn Lloyd-Jones defines** *praus***:** Quoted in John Stott, *The Message of the Sermon on the Mount* (Westmont, IL: IVP Academic, 1985).

37   **A rabbi once said:** Quoted in Philip Yancey, *Reaching for the Invisible God* (Grand Rapids: Zondervan, 2000), 93.

38   **Greek scholar Fritz Rienecker has this definition for** *praus***:** Fritz Rienecker, *A Linguistic Key to the Greek New Testament: Romans-Revelation* (Grand Rapids: Zondervan, 1976), 139.

39 **James Montgomery Boice defines *praus*:** James Montgomery Boice, *The Sermon on the Mount: Matthew 5-7* (Ada, MI: Baker Books, 2006), 33.

40 **In her words, she wished:** Quoted in Bethany Haley Williams, *The Color of Grace: How One Woman's Brokenness Brought Healing and Hope to Child Survivors of War* (Brentwood, TN: Howard Books, 2016), 98.

41 **one of the finest faith commitments I know:** Patrick Sookhdeo, *Heroes of our Faith: Inspiration and Strength for Daily Living* (McLean, VA: Isaac Publishing, 2012), March 15.

CHAPTER 4

44 **Theologian Paul Tillich was right:** Paul Tillich, *Dynamics of Faith* (New York: HarperOne, 2009), 1.

45 **Dwight Moody said that your character:** William R. Moody, *D.L. Moody* (Chicago: Moody Press, 2013).

46 **Abigail Adams:** David McCullough, *John Adams* (New York: Simon and Schuster, 2008), 310.

46 **President George W. Bush:** *PBS News Hour*, "President Bush's Speech," last modified July 9, 2002, https://www.pbs.org/newshour/show/president-bushs-speech.

47 **Niccolò Paganini was in concert:** Steve May, *Your Life is Now*, "Paganini and One String," last

modified March 20, 2017, https://stevemay.com/
paganini-one-string/.

50   **A group of American ministers:** Arnold A.
Dallimore, *Spurgeon: A Biography* (Edinburgh:
Banner of Truth, 1985).

CHAPTER 5

53   **A man built a pyramid:** Sheena Goodyear and
Allie Jaynes, *CBC Radio*, "Phoenix man says
he built the world's largest coin pyramid out of
pennies," last modified June 18, 2019, https://
www.cbc.ca/radio/asithappens/as-it-happens-
tuesday-edition-1.5179826/phoenix-man-says-
he-built-the-world-s-largest-coin-pyramid-out-of-
pennies-1.5179827.

53   **A man in Spain:** Wade Sheridan, *UPI*, "Artisan
blue cheese sells for Guinness record of over
$16,000," last modified June 20, 2019, https://www.
upi.com/Odd_News/
2019/06/20/Artisan-blue-cheese-sells-for-Guinness-
record-of-over-16000/5831561047977/.

53   **Another man fit:** Ben Hooper, *UPI*, "Man fits 146
blueberries in his mouth for Guinness record," last
modified June 17, 2019, https://www.upi.com/Odd_
News/2019/06/17/Man-fits-146-blueberries-in-his-
mouth-for-Guinness-record/2531560795039/.

54   **And veterinarians removed:** *KXAN*, "Veterinarian
removes 19 pacifiers from stomach of bulldog,"
last modified June 22, 2019, https://www.kxan.
com/news/veterinarian-removes-19-pacifiers-from-

stomach-of-bulldog/.

54   **Ethicist Lewis Smedes:** Lewis B. Smedes, *Forgive and Forget: Healing the Hurts We Don't Deserve* (New York: HarperCollins, 1984).

56   **Frederick Buechner:** Frederick Buechner, *Wishful Thinking* (New York: Harper and Row, 1973) 2.

58   **During the depths of the Cold War:** Dorothy Kelley Patterson, *A Handbook for Ministers' Wives: Sharing the Blessing of Your Marriage, Family, and Home* (Nashville: B&H Books, 2002), 226.

60   **When the great astronomer Copernicus:** James S. Hewitt, Ed., *Illustrations Unlimited: A Topical Collection of Hundreds of Stories, Quotations, & Humor* (Carol Stream, IL: Tyndale House Publishers, 1988), 346.

CHAPTER 6

63   ***There are three tame ducks*:** Public domain. Generally attributed to Kenneth Kaufman.

64   **Greek scholar Fritz Rienecker:** *A Linguistic Key to the Greek New Testament: Romans-Revelation* (Grand Rapids: Zondervan, 1976).

65   **Kierkegaard was right:** Soren Kierkegaard, *Purity of Heart is to Will One Thing* (Jersey City, NJ: Start Publishing, 2013).

65   **Philosopher Martin Heidegger:** Martin Heidegger, *Being and Time*. 1927 (New York: Harper and Row, 1962, Reprint).

65 **Winston Churchill in June of 1941:** Winston S. Churchill, *The Grand Alliance (The Second World War: Volume III* (Boston: Houghton Mifflin, 1986), 331.

65 **Brilliant scholar and author William Barclay:** William Barclay, Day by Day With William Barclay: Selected Readings for Daily Reflection (Peabody, MA: Hendrickson Publishers, 2003), 44.

69 **A crash once closed:** *CBS Denver*, "Google Maps Mishap: Nearly 100 Drivers End Up Stuck In Muddy Field Near DIA," last modified June 27, 2019, https://denver.cbslocal.com/2019/06/27/google-maps-detour-drivers-muddy-field-denver-airport/.

CHAPTER 7

71 **A friend sent me these first-grade proverbs:** *Lee's Latest*, "Proverbs ... Kids' Endings," http://www.primepuzzle.com/leeslatest/proverbs.html.

72 **It has been estimated that in the last 3,400 years:** Chris Hedges, "What Every Person Should Know About War," *The New York Times*, last modified July 6, 2003, https://www.nytimes.com/2003/07/06/books/chapters/what-every-person-should-know-about-war.html.

73 **Actress Sophia Loren told *USA Today*:** Craig Brian Larson, *Perfect Illustrations for Every Topic and Occasion* (Carol Stream, IL: Tyndale House Publishers, 2002), 8.

74   **Musician Paul Simon:** Anthony DeCurtis, *In Other Words: Artists Talk About Life and Work* (Milwaukee: Hal Leonard, 2006), 126.

74   **Dwight Moody gave a Bible to a friend:** Henry Gariepy, *Daily Meditations on Golden Texts of the Bible* (Grand Rapids, MI: Eerdmans, 2004), 261.

75   **H. G. Wells was right:** Widely attributed to H. G. Wells.

77   **Consider John Wesley:** John Wesley, *The Works of John Wesley*, 3d ed., complete and unabridged (Grand Rapids, MI: Baker Books, 2007), 1:22.

78   **Francis of Assisi was riding:** Arnaldo Fortoni, *Francis of Assisi*, transl. Helen Moak (New York: Crossroad, 1992), 211.

CHAPTER 8

81   **Christians are the most persecuted religious group in the world:** Zelda Caldwell, "Christians are the most persecuted group in the world, study says," *Aleteia*, last modified May 6, 2019, https://aleteia.org/2019/05/06/christians-are-most-persecuted-group-in-the-world-study-says/.

82   **According to Gary Bauer:** Cited by Jennifer Wishon, "Global Persecution Report: 'Christians Are the Most Persecuted . . . and It's Accelerating,'" *CBN News*, last modified April 30, 2019, https://www1.cbn.com/cbnnews/politics/2019/april/global-persecution-report-christians-are-the-most-persecuted-and-its-accelerating.

82   **While 30 percent of the world's population:**
      John L. Allen, Jr., *The Global War on Christians:
      Dispatches from the Front Lines of Anti-Christian
      Persecution* (New York: Image, 2013), 9, 33, 44,
      35.

82   **When atheist Sam Harris:** Sam Harris, "Science
      Must Destroy Religion," *samharris.org*, last
      modified January 2, 2006, https://samharris.org/
      science-must-destroy-religion/, accessed 9 July
      2019.

82   **religion is not just irrelevant:** For more, see Jim
      Denison, "How to respond when skeptics claim our
      faith is dangerous," *Denison Forum*, last modified
      January 28, 2019, https://www.denisonforum.org/
      columns/daily-article/respond-skeptics-claim-faith-
      dangerous/.

83   **William Barclay:** William Barclay, *The Gospel
      of Matthew, rev. ed.,* The Daily Study Bible Series
      (Philadelphia, Pennsylvania: Westminster Press,
      1975), 1:112.

84   **Seventy million believers:** Kath Martin, "'70
      million Christians' martyred for their faith since
      Jesus walked the earth," *Christianity Today*, last
      modified June 25, 2014, https://www.christiantoday.
      com/article/70-million-christians-martyred-faith-
      since-jesus-walked-earth/38403.htm.

84   **More believers were martyred:** Justin D. Long,
      John Mark Ministries, "More Martyrs Now than
      Then? Examining the real situation of martyrdom,"
      last modified August 1997, http://www.jmm.org.au/

articles/2904.htm.

84 **Thomas à Kempis observed:** Thomas à Kempis, *The Imitation of Christ*, rev. ed. (Notre Dame, IN: Christian Classics, 2017).

87 **Justin, one of the earliest martyrs:** Justin Martyr, *First and Second Apologies* (Beloved Publishing, 2015).

87 **Martyr Jim Elliott:** Elisabeth Elliot, *Shadow of the Almighty: The Life and Testament of Jim Elliot* (Peabody, MA: Hendrickson Publishers, 2008), 15.

89 **The *Epistle to Diognetus*:** Mathetes, *The Epistle of Mathetes to Diognetus* (Beloved Publishing, 2016), 14.

89 **Sundar Singh:** Rebecca Jane Parker, *Sádhu Sundar Singh, called of God* (Ulan Press, 2012).

CHAPTER 9

91 **By 1976, nearly four million:** "Number of Abortions - Abortion Counters," last modified July 12, 2019, http://www.numberofabortions.com/.

92 **Today, one in five:** *Gallup News*, "Majority of Americans Remain Supportive of Euthanasia, https://news.gallup.com/poll/.../majority-americans-remain-supportive-euthanasia.aspx.

92 **American Psychological Association:** "Task Forces: Consensual Non-Monogamy Task Force,"

American Psychological Association, https://www.apadivisions.org/division-44/leadership/task-forces/index.

92   **a movie about a sexual relationship:** "Dolphin Lover," *imdb.com*, https://www.imdb.com/title/tt4286742.

92   **percentage of Americans with no religious affiliation:** Daniel Cox and Robert P. Jones, *PRRI*, "America's Changing Religious Identity," last modified September 6, 2017, https://www.prri.org/research/american-religious-landscape-christian-religiously-unaffiliated/.

92   **those who describe themselves as Protestants:** *Gallup*, "In Depth: Topics A to Z: Religion," https://news.gallup.com/poll/1690/religion.aspx.

94   **The Chinese theologian Watchman Nee:** Watchman Nee, *The Normal Christian Life* (London: Witness and Testimony Publishers, 1958) 134–5.

Made in the USA
Las Vegas, NV
23 April 2022

47918094R00108